Social Sciences

We live in a world that is frequently characterized by change. What are these changes? Are they so radical? Do changes also bring uncertainties as well as new opportunities? How can we understand the things that matter? These are the questions with which the social sciences engage. The social sciences are about people and the relationship between individuals and the social world in which we live. Some contemporary debates have a long history, whereas others are expressed differently in the age of new technologies and the Internet.

Social Sciences offers an introduction to the big debates within the social sciences and to the ways of thinking and of dealing with what matters, which the social sciences employ. It introduces some of the important concepts and claims that promote understanding of recent discussions of identity, citizenship, social divisions, consumption and class, gender, race and ethnicity, the role of the media and the impact of globalization.

This book will be of particular interest to students wanting to bridge the gap between Access courses or A levels and social sciences degrees, and for those who are considering studying the social sciences at undergraduate level and want to know more about what might be involved, as well as to those who just want to think more systematically about issues of social and political concern and develop some of the tools of critical analysis.

Kath Woodward is Senior Lecturer in Sociology at the Open University.

Social Sciences

The big issues

Kath Woodward

Routledge
Taylor & Francis Group

LONDON AND NEW YORK

First published 2003
by Routledge
11 New Fetter Lane, London EC4P 4EE

Simultaneously published in the USA and Canada
by Routledge
29 West 35th Street, New York, NY 10001

Reprinted 2004 (twice)

Routledge is an imprint of the Taylor & Francis Group

© 2003 Kath Woodward

Typeset in Times New Roman by
Keystroke, Jacaranda Lodge, Wolverhampton

Printed and bound in Great Britain by
The Cromwell Press, Trowbridge, Wiltshire

British Library Cataloguing in Publication Data
A catalogue record for this book is available from the British Library

Library of Congress Cataloging in Publication Data
A catalog record for this book has been requested

ISBN 0–415–30079–7 (hb)
ISBN 0–415–30080–0 (pb)

For Steve, Richard, Tamsin, Jack and Sophie and my sister Sarah

Contents

Illustrations

Plates

Figures

Tables

Acknowledgements

The author and publishers would like to thank Time Warner Books UK for permission to reprint 'The Fat Black Woman Goes Shopping' from *The Fat Black Woman's Poems* by Grace Nichols, first published by Virago, London, 1984; Time Warner Books UK.

Acknowledgement is also made to the following for photographs and permission to reproduce illustrations: Empics, Nottingham for plates 5.1, 5.2, 6.2 and 6.3; Popperfoto for plates 6.1 (courtesy: Jeff Christensen/Reuters/Popperfoto) and 6.4 (courtesy: Andrea Comas/Reuters/Popperfoto); HMSO (Crown copyright) for figures 4.1 and 4.3 and for tables 4.1, 4.2 and 5.1.

Thanks to Sylvia Lay-Flurrie for her help with the typing.

Chapter 1

Introduction

Getting started

Introduction

This is a book about big issues. Big questions about world politics, environmental degradation, social and economic inequality and cultural change inform debates in the social sciences. Recent developments range from concerns about global terrorism, which has replaced conflicts between nation states as a major cause of anxiety across the entire world, to the growth of transnational corporations. Change is taking place with a new intensity through the progress of technological developments. These are issues which have arisen as a result of some of the major changes that have taken place in recent years in power relationships, in global politics and economics as well as through the development of new technologies and working practices. In a sense this is also a book about little issues, in that the debates that are the focus of the social sciences are also the concerns of individuals in our everyday lives. These are the big issues that concern us in our daily routines. These everyday matters include our sense of who we are in our exchanges with friends, family and in our local communities and at work. Dealing with health, welfare and ill health, shopping and in the leisure activities in which we might engage, all matter, as well as the global, big issues relating to big business, corporate finance, international politics, conflicts between states, environmental degradation and risk. My concern in this book is to show the links between the two, between global events and everyday experience and, in particular, to introduce some of the ways in which the social sciences help us make sense of everyday life and offer different ways of understanding what matters. These are the big issues, the things that matter, the areas of experience which are changing and those about which there is most debate and contention. The social sciences offer critical ways of thinking and of making sense of social, political, cultural and economic life. The approach taken in this book is to highlight some of the concepts of the social sciences and ways of classifying and understanding different social phenomena and to introduce some of the questions that the social sciences pose. Knowing which questions to ask is a most important stage in the process of doing social science. Getting started involves asking questions.

Change, and especially the speed with which some changes in the social, economic, political and cultural patterns of our daily lives are taking place, have characterized the contemporary world. Within a single generation it is possible to trace very different patterns of family life, experiences of paid work, of sexual relations and patterns of ethnic and cultural diversity. Exploring the extent to which such changes are taking place is crucial to understanding the extent of change and to moving towards an understanding of these changes. What sort of changes are taking place in the contemporary world? Where could we look to find out what's happening?

Changing places; changing times

Demographic changes have had enormous impact upon our daily lives. Demography involves all aspects of human populations, including growth and decline, different patterns of movement across the globe, births and deaths, the ratio of women to men, young to old, ill health and dependency. One of the ways of accessing information about demographic changes is to look at the official statistical data produced by government-sponsored sources. In the UK there is a range of such sources, including the annual surveys produced as the publications *Social Trends* and *British Social Attitudes*. Some of the evidence cited in this book draws upon such sources.

Population changes include not only an increase in overall numbers, but an increase in numbers of people within particular age categories, for example the elderly in most western countries and, in some cases, a decrease in other age groups, notably the under sixteens. These trends raise some important questions about how care of the elderly is to be financed and organized if there is a declining working population. Population changes in countries like the UK have involved both a shift towards an ageing population and migration replacing births as the major cause of population growth (*Social Trends* 2002). The growth of more multicultural societies raises issues about national identities and demands a rethinking of some traditional ideas about who we are and about social and political policies.

Fertility patterns have changed in other ways as well as a declining birth rate. Not only has there been a decline in the number of babies born in most European countries, but also later marriage, women's increased participation in higher education and in the labour market and the availability of contraception have all contributed to an increase in the average age of mothers at birth, as well as a decline in the fertility rate. However, the proportion of teenage girls becoming pregnant and going on to deliver a live baby is high, especially in the UK. In fact, the UK is the European capital of teenage pregnancies and births. There are relatively high rates of births outside marriage in other northern European countries, although rates are falling slightly. Births to teenage mothers are most likely to take place outside marriage. For example, in 2000, 90 per cent of births to women aged under 20 in England and Wales occurred outside marriage (*Social Trends* 2002: 47).

What constitutes a family is changing. The traditional notion of a married couple living together with their children as the dominant form of household has been transformed. The proportion of UK households comprising a couple with dependent children fell from 35 per cent of all households in 1971 to 23 per cent in 2001, whilst the proportion of people living alone doubled from 6 per cent to 12 per cent over the same period. Patterns of partnership have changed since the mid-1970s. Although the majority of adults in the UK do get married, marriage rates in the west have fallen drastically, whilst numbers of those cohabiting have risen sharply. The year 2001 saw the first increase in the number of marriages in the UK for nearly ten years but the overall trend has been downward. There were 390,000 first marriages in the UK in 1970 and only 179,000 in 1999. Although, for many, cohabitation is the precursor to marriage, it is not for all, and increasing numbers of children are born to unmarried couples: 40 per cent in 2002 (*The Guardian* 18 October 2002: 25).

Divorce rates have continued to rise. UK divorce rates rose dramatically in 1971 and 1972 following the Divorce Reform Act of 1969, which introduced the irretrievable breakdown of marriage as the sole grounds for divorce, removing the concepts of 'guilty party' and 'matrimonial offence'. In the 1970s and early 1980s the proportion of divorces granted to wives increased, whereas before 1969, more petitions had been brought by husbands. In 1999, 70 per cent of decrees were awarded to women. Some of these changes have led to different roles for women and for men and significantly changing expectations of relationships and of family life, including the ways in which children are brought up.

The UK, along with most societies in the contemporary world, is a multi-ethnic society with diverse practices that vary across ethnic groups. However, there are overall indicators of change over time, of movement towards changes in couple relationships and in childbearing, which might suggest that there are shifts in relations between women and men. How far these changes indicate shifts in power relations between women and men is debatable. Women are more likely to be participating in the labour market and to have fewer children and to postpone childbearing; women are more likely to leave unsatisfactory marriages and teenage girls may be more likely to reject the stigma that was attached to lone and early parenthood.

These demographic shifts are linked to other social, economic, cultural and political changes. The labour market has been transformed by changing patterns of production and consumption and, especially, by the move away from heavy manufacturing industry, characterized by full-time male employment, towards an emphasis on service sector industries and new technologies. Over the last twenty years of the twentieth century in the UK there was a move from a third of men in employment being in manufacturing industry to just over a fifth. The number of women in the labour force has risen, for example from 10 million in 1971 to 13.2 million in 2001 in a UK workforce of 27.3 million.

As these changes are transforming people's everyday lives, so have there been considerable shifts in sources of information for understanding the changes that are taking place. There has been a questioning of traditional sources of authority, such as religious leaders, politicians, doctors, teachers, as well as the opening up of new forms of access to knowledge, for example through the Internet and other sites of the mass media. Increasingly people in the west turn to self-help sources of advice and guidance in coming to terms with the changes that are taking place in their own lives, especially in terms of personal relationships. Think about the number of places where you might find advice on how to conduct personal relationships: in the problem pages of magazines and newspapers, in television programmes, in advertisements, in books and on the Internet, as well as through self-help groups. The plethora of media texts, including media coverage of personal counselling, translated into the popular discourses of self-help guidance of magazines and television shows, all challenge the authority of more traditional sources of expertise. Self-help advice saturates a whole range of media locations. The media have assumed enormous importance as a source of knowledge and information and in transforming social relations. In many ways this can be read positively as offering much more democratic access to a range of sources of expertise and knowledge. Traditional sources of expertise through the institutions of the state and of medicine, science and established religion are supplemented by an abundance of alternative and complementary sources of knowledge, involving the new expertise of self-help and relationship counselling. This is not to say that there are not significant continuities, as well as expressions of the desire to find sources of certainty and security in a world that appears to be presenting so many changing experiences. Indeed the tensions between change and continuity, between fluidity and security are what inform much of the thinking in the contemporary social sciences. The social sciences have to address the changes taking place at different levels, covering the personal and the global areas of experience, in order to identify trends and to provide explanatory frameworks which can inform policies and practices.

A case study: rags to riches, social transformation?

In 2002, a black British teenager who had been asked to leave his school – being described as 'rude, disruptive and unmanageable' (Ahmed 2002: 3) – received what must have seemed like incredible good luck. The teenager who had been wandering the streets of inner-city London, beginning to engage in some near criminal activities and consorting with petty criminals, was transported to one of the UK's top public schools (that is a selective, independent, fee-paying school) to see how he would cope. Fifteen-year-old Ryan had been forced to leave his previous school in South London after several disagreements with teachers and a refusal on his part to attend school regularly and devote himself to his studies. After the head teacher of the school had written many times to Ryan's mother warning that if her son did not agree to leave he would be expelled from the school, the situation had reached crisis point. Media coverage of the story does not mention a father and Ryan is described as living in a council house in a poor part of London, suggesting an inauspicious start to life and that his chances of academic success might be slim. The fairy godmother in this case was a television company owned by the Labour politician Trevor Phillips and the motive for engineering this almost magical removal of a person at the bottom end of the social scale to a position somewhere near the top, was not entirely altruistic. The television company paid the £15,000-a-year fees for Ryan to attend Downside Roman Catholic boarding school in Somerset, in order to film his progress over a period of twelve months and broadcast the outcome on Channel 4. The boarding school offered not only small classes but also a wide range of activities and pastoral support.

What was the outcome of this Cinderella-like experience? Was it one of transformation?

> He excelled. Ryan, 15, is now studying for GCSEs, came top in Latin and biology and is a leading member of the school rugby team. His report card put him in the top third of pupils at the school.
>
> (Ahmed 2002: 3)

The story makes good newspaper copy because of its apparent happy ending in that Ryan's experience is positive. As Ryan is reported as saying, 'A few months ago I would have been spray painting graffiti. Now I'm sitting 10 GCSEs' (ibid.: 3). Having been given both the chance to benefit from small classes of sixteen pupils, rather than over thirty as at his previous state school, and support through the provision of an extensive range of activities including sports, which are well resourced and highly valued, he has been successful. The Channel 4 television programme broadcast in 2003 was slightly more ambivalent about the outcome. However, it makes a good story, which can be used to illustrate many of the main aspects of social science enquiry and demands that we address some of the key questions posed by social scientists.

This story is about educational experience and the impact of education on people's lives. It is also a story of transformation from failure to success, almost in the manner of a fantasy tale of rags to riches. Of course, we do not as yet know the outcome in terms of Ryan's adult life and achievements, although the television company has agreed to pay his school fees until he leaves school at 18.

Although this story seems to be about what looks like one person's good luck story, an individual narrative of change, it is also about much wider social issues. This story illustrates some important dimensions of social scientific analysis. So what can the social sciences contribute to our understanding of what is going on here? What sort of questions do we need to ask? What additional information do we need in order to make sense of this situation? There are a series of questions around which we can organize our discussion.

Firstly, how can we locate this individual story in the context of wider narrative and a broader social picture? Is Ryan's experience in any way typical of others of his generation? If it is, which are the factors that matter? Is it where he lives, his gender, education policies, ethnicity or ways in which race is perceived? This might involve a deeper investigation of the issues, in order to suggest reasons for Ryan's previous poor performance at school. The case study is used as an example of how we can attempt to make sense of our lives and to explain different experiences by using some of the frameworks provided by the social sciences. How do we need to organize the information we have in order to provide an explanation and to set Ryan's individual experience in the wider social context? What else do we need to know about educational opportunities and the society in which Ryan lives? This looks like lots of questions! However, what is important is starting with the questions and then identifying what counts.

What makes education interesting?

Education has particular importance in the contemporary world in relation to the changing demands for knowledge and its applications, at a time of rapid change and development in both sources of knowledge and in the transmission of ideas.

Background to the UK

In the second half of the twentieth century there was a huge expansion of education, with more children staying on at school and an emphasis on social mobility, that is the possibility of children from working-class homes achieving a higher level of occupation and earnings than their parents. The initial emphasis was on social *class*, with educational policies directed at increasing the participation of working-class children and young people in the educational system. The path towards social mobility and equal opportunities has not been entirely smooth and even, however, and over this period there have been moves, for example in the 1980s, towards greater parental choice and the application of market principles to education. This has enabled middle-class families to adopt particular strategies to their own benefit. For example such families can send their children to particularly popular and successful state schools by exercising their choice, even by moving into more appropriate catchment areas, or being able to take their children some distance to attend the best school. As a result they are able to ensure that certain advantages are transmitted to their own children. These advantages can be accessed through such strategies, or through the probably more expensive means of sending their children to fee-paying schools.

Increasingly education has to be seen as lifelong learning and is not confined to the school ages. In the UK school attendance is compulsory between the ages of 5 and 16, but the majority of young people stay on until 18 and now many continue with further training. Many also start school before the age of 5. In 2001, 63 per cent of 3 and 4-year-olds attended school, compared with only 21 per cent in 1971. In 2001, of the 6.3 million people of working age in the UK who were studying towards a qualification, over half were aged between 16 and 24 while a quarter were aged 35 or over (*Social Trends* 2002: 53).

The UK has a system of education which incorporates private, fee-paying schools, called public schools, and state-funded, free education. The continuance of this division between free schooling and the often more prestigious and selective, fee-paying sector remains highly contentious and throws into relief one of the main areas of debate in contemporary education, the question of inequality. Inequality has many other dimensions, notably those arising from the influence of class, gender and ethnicity. From gender inequalities having mainly concerned the underperformance of girls and young women, especially in mathematics, physics and chemistry, concern has been expressed more volubly in recent years about the underperformance of boys. By the late 1990s girls were outperforming boys at age 16 across all ethnic groups in terms of the standard of those staying on in full-time education to take A levels. However, it has to be noted that there has been a steady improvement for all young people. (This itself has been the cause of some contention, with claims that examinations have become less challenging or even that results have been 'fixed'). The proportion of young women in the UK achieving two or more A levels (or equivalent qualification) has increased by approximately 20 per cent since 1996 to 39 per cent in 2000. For young men there has been an increase, but a more modest one by 14 per cent, to 31 per cent.

Using the qualifications at the end of compulsory schooling, the General Certificate in Secondary Education (GCSE), to examine the differences between ethnic groups, at school, indicates significant differences in achievement. Using the standard of five or more GCSE grades A to C, there is a similar pattern to other levels of achievement. Using this standard, in 2001, 6 per cent of black young men left school with no such qualifications, whereas only 3 per cent of white young women did and there were no recorded numbers of Indian young men in this category. The data indicate 15 per cent of young men and 14 per cent of young women in this category of low achievers who are classified as 'other groups' and who did not disclose their ethnic group (*Social Trends* 2002: 62). African Caribbean males are the most likely to be permanently excluded from school (ibid.: 63). African Caribbean young people have not, on the whole, shared in the advances in the achievement of higher educational qualifications which have been made in recent years in the UK. It is important to note that, whilst this evidence is drawn from official statistical sources, it does have significant drawbacks. It may represent broad trends and patterns of achievement or underachievement, but we need to ask further questions about the data. *Social Trends*' evidence links Indian, Pakistani and Bangladeshi students together in one category for some of its tables. This overlooks the very distinct differences between members of these communities, for example in terms of class and culture. Similarly, black is used to cover African Caribbean and those of more recent African family history. Again, the general grouping may obscure some important differences. There are big differences between Indian families with parents in professional employment and Bangladeshi families whose socio-economic position is relatively disadvantaged. Class privilege, indicated by the higher levels of achievement overall for middle-class children and young people across the divisions of gender and ethnicity, is difficult to disentangle from the evidence of gender and ethnicity. It is also worth noting that ethnic category is not always indicated and that there are reasons for people not wanting to disclose their ethnic identity. This may also contribute to difficulties in evaluating such evidence. However, it is cited here to indicate trends and to set the context for the discussion of the case study.

Ryan's educational story is about inequality and social divisions. It is a good story and a newsworthy one because it tells of a disadvantaged person making good and transforming into a successful achiever. Even if the story does not accord with anyone's actual experience it relates to contemporary life and has the appeal of a narrative of transformation. The message appears to be that transformation is possible and final outcomes are not fixed; education can have an effect and make changes. The person who has suffered inequality in this story becomes the equal of others who have been more privileged. From being disadvantaged and deviant a young person becomes successful and integrated into society. He not only belongs he is also successful, as a result of a different educational experience.

Education receives a great deal of media coverage for a variety of reasons. Everyone has some experience of the education system, which means that everyone has some investment and some memories of their own experiences – whether negative or positive. Most importantly, education is closely tied to the demands of contemporary societies in which *knowledge* is the key motor of change, a creator of wealth and crucial element of social advancement. This is apparent in the work of Daniel Bell writing in the 1970s about post-industrial societies of the crucial economic role of those who create and circulate knowledge, more so than goods and products (Bell 1976). More recently, Charles Leadbeater (1999) has argued about the centrality of knowledge as the main source of innovation, competitiveness and productivity.

Why is education important? Firstly, education is a crucial component of the experience of young people in the contemporary world. In western countries education is a right, although in the developing world it may be more of a privilege and is not easily accessed by all. In the west all young people between approximately 5 and 16 attend school or are educated in some approved way, and many remain in full-time education to 18 or even 21, with increasing numbers attending higher education institutions. Increasingly education is seen as a lifelong project. Secondly, educational spending is a significant part of government expenditure and one that receives a great deal of public attention. Thirdly, educational qualifications are necessary for full participation in social, cultural and economic life. There may be a few exceptions, such as the superstars of professional football, pop music and other areas of celebrity life, but for the majority of the population education is important in order to participate fully in any modern society. This is even more the case in a rapidly changing world where knowledge is often the most valuable and valued commodity in the creation of wealth; in the 'knowledge society' of the contemporary world.

- Education is important for individuals. In developed societies educational qualifications and skills enable people to make choices and to participate fully in the society in which they live where knowledge is so vital.
- Education is a key component in social policy; an essential element in government spending and thus has considerable social and political importance.

- Thus education links the personal and individual to the social and public areas of experience.

Education and inequality

If education is one of the keys to full participation in social and economic life it is clear that educational policies are often directed at redressing inequalities and at promoting greater equality through the provision of equal opportunities. If those who might be otherwise disadvantaged are given the chance to develop their skills and greater understanding and knowledge they can achieve greater equality. Thus education has been concerned with equal opportunities and the idea that it provides a means of eliminating or at least reducing social inequalities. The means of achieving greater social justice, for example through the implementation of educational policies that promote equal opportunities, is a strongly contested area within the social sciences and within politics. What do we mean by social justice in this context?

ACTIVITY

Think about your own experience of education for a moment. Can you think of any examples of injustices in relation to your education?

COMMENT

Obviously there will be different responses to this question and your reaction will depend on your own position. Age is an important factor. For some people there may be strong memories of the injustice of having to leave school early because of lack of financial support within the family for them to stay on. There may have been parental expectations that it would be more important to get a job than to study any further or simply no money to support you in education. In the past, it was often expected that girls would marry and therefore not need to pursue their studies. Boys would need qualifications, as they would be the breadwinners. Similarly you may have been discouraged from studying subjects seen as more appropriate for the other gender. Some single-sex schools offered only a very limited curriculum, for example there were no science laboratories in some girls' schools. For others, there may be memories of the unfairness of selective examinations like the 11-plus in the UK. According to this system of selection, children were classified at the age of 11 as either academic and able to benefit from a grammar school education, or they would be expected to take more vocational and less academic subjects and be unlikely to go on to higher education and sent to a secondary modern school. People may recall having been unable to attend the school chosen by their parents or the school where all their friends or even older siblings went, because school rolls were full. In some cases an inner-city school may have been beset by social problems that the school could not redress and the learning process may have been greatly impeded by the presence of troubled and disruptive children in the classroom.

Most of these examples relate to the structure of education and to factors mostly outside the control of individuals, involving policies at a particular time rather than the agency of individuals. If any of your experiences of injustice were of being bullied or picked on, you may think that some action on the part of one or more individuals was involved and the injustice could not be laid at the door of the education system. You may have experienced oppression based on race, ethnicity, gender or perhaps a disability or physical characteristic. Although individuals may have perpetrated the injustices, there are likely to have been social aspects involved. There are other factors at play, such as the culture of the local community or even the wider society, the social circumstances of those responsible for acts of hostility and bullying and the policies of the school for dealing with such occurrences.

Social justice can be interpreted in different ways but in these examples it involves fair treatment, freedom from oppression and marginalization and equal access to resources. Justice involves some equality of outcomes through fair treatment. If we think of justice as involving equal outcomes it may be very different from advocating equal treatment of all concerned at the outset, since some children, for example, will need special treatment. There are two issues here, equality and difference, both of which are major concerns within the social sciences. The key point about social justice in relation to education is that it focuses on equality and inequality and the need to provide some explanation of why children are not equal at the start of their educational careers. What makes them unequal? How can we use the case study of the black teenager discussed above to explore what sort of divisions make for inequality and upon which social factors do social scientists focus when looking for explanations of inequality in such cases?

Making sense of the story

We have a limited range of material to work with but firstly we need to sort out what is important. What categories and concepts are important? What is the most important aspect of disadvantage which Ryan experienced before he was sent to a well-resourced independent school? He came from a family without the resources to send him to an expensive fee-paying school. He lives on a council estate and his mother may be a lone parent, which might indicate some disadvantage in terms of family income. (The media coverage makes no reference to his father.) All of these are indicators of relative lack of wealth and affluence, which suggest that Ryan's *class* position could be a relevant factor in determining his life chances. Without the benefactor of a television company, Ryan's family would not be able to give him such a privileged education. Class covers a person's socio-economic grouping. Class is defined in many different ways by social scientists and in recent years has been a less popular category of classifying social divisions. Class focuses on economic position, for example in relation to the labour market and a person's position within the economic system. Class includes access to resources and is a crucial factor in understanding social divisions. In recent years, more emphasis has been given to other aspects of difference, such as race and ethnicity, gender, sexuality and place and some social scientists have used the notion of 'lifestyle' rather than class to incorporate a wider range of factors. However, class is a very important way of positioning people in relation to their social and economic standing in relation to others; to those with whom they share a class position in relation to those who are classified differently. Discussion of the concept of class is taken up in more detail in Chapter 4 but it is signalled here as an important concept within the social sciences, which has a long history and makes significant contributions to debates about equality and inequality and the ways in which societies are divided.

Another significant aspect of Ryan's case is his *gender*. As a black, teenage boy, in 2002, he belongs to a category that has been identified as underachieving in terms of education in the UK. In recent years, arguments have moved from focusing on the underachievement of girls, especially in subjects such as physics, to a focus on the relatively low achievement of boys, especially African and African Caribbean boys. The term gender is used in preference to sex because of the social and cultural connotations which it carries. Although there is no clear-cut distinction between the two, sex and gender are closely related, but gender allows for an accommodation of all the social and cultural meanings that go with being assigned the gender of female or male, rather than seeing these attributes as purely biologically given and fixed. Feminist critics have pointed to the primacy of gender, that is the expected behaviour and power structures that accompany particular gender divisions, in organizing society. Gender is a key factor shaping life chances and is closely linked to other aspects of difference. The main point about theories that foreground gender as a key dimension of difference is that they see power as operating through gender difference, significantly in the power which men are able to exert over women in patriarchal societies. In recent years the emphasis has shifted from a focus on women, whereby gender is seen as being about women, to an examination of how masculinity is constructed and experienced. This has particular resonance in the above case study, since Ryan's original experience of school seems to accord with the recent low performance of some boys, linked to a masculinity that stresses deviance rather than conformity, especially in terms of academic work.

Here gender is linked to class and to *race* and *ethnicity* as factors that shape Ryan's life chances. Ethnicity includes the language, customs, rituals and practices that are associated with a particular group of people, the identity that they share. The term race, sometimes expressed as 'race', is used in the social sciences to cover the social identities that are often based on visible differences between people and possibly some physical characteristics they may share. The term race is sometimes preferred because it retains a political dimension, whereas ethnicity is mostly descriptive, and race allows for a recognition of *racism* which is often involved in the relations between people from different ethnic groups. The use of inverted commas, or 'scare quotes', around 'race' allows for a focus on racial difference that shows that the concept is not fixed and biologically rooted, but is a dynamic, socially influenced category. The UK is a multicultural society characterized by citizens from diverse ethnic groups. Multiculturalism and diversity are outcomes of change in the contemporary world in which there has been massive movement of peoples over the last century and especially in recent years with political upheavals following the breakup of the USSR and events in what was Eastern Europe as well as Africa. Migration has led to the advantages of multiculturalism and the enrichment of diversity, but it is also distinguished by hostility and racism. Migrants are not always well received and racism is also a feature of most western societies like the UK. As a black teenager, where 'black' most likely means African Caribbean British, Ryan is part of an ethnic group that has been subject to racial discrimination in the UK. This is taken up in more detail in Chapter 5, but it is signposted here as one of the important ways of addressing social divisions and as a key aspect of social change.

Another relevant issue is *place*. Ryan lives on an inner-city housing estate and the school to which he is moved is in rural Somerset. Again, some of the other social divisions, namely gender, class and ethnicity, operate along with place to shape Ryan's experience and his participation in education. Place offers an important dimension of social difference and contributes to our understanding of social divisions. The place where we live and the place we come from play key roles in shaping our identities and our life chances. The increased movement of people through not only migration across the globe, but also greater mobility required within countries, for example by employment, leads to an emphasis on place as important in understanding social change.

Ryan's success on the rugby field at his new school would imply that he is able-bodied and healthy. *Disability* is another aspect of difference that can lead to exclusion and inequality. Physical and mental impairments carry social meanings. The experience of disability may be shaped by social factors, including the physical environment, how it is organized, whether or not it is structured to facilitate mobility and freedom for everyone, and social and cultural attitudes, which may greatly constrain those suffering some impairment. Understandings of disability may accord greater or lesser weight to social factors, although there may still be limitations which lie outside social meanings. Ryan's story illustrates the relationship between what is innate and natural and what is the outcome of social matters. In this context we are thinking about the relationship between the *body* and the environment, between what could be called 'inner nature' and 'outer nature'. Inner nature is the body, its biology, physical and psychological aspects and outer nature is the environment in which we live, which includes social organization and structures. Ryan's story was publicized as engaging with what was called the '*nature versus nurture*' debate, which is a shorthand and simplified summary of the tension between the 'inner nature' of embodied characteristics, skills and propensities and the 'nurture' of education in this instance. The 'experiment' of moving a young person from an educational environment in which he was not succeeding to one in which he would be given maximum support and advantages was carried out to see if it was possible to transform an underachiever into a successful student. The failure of such an experiment might suggest that academic success is predetermined, genetically fixed and that 'inner nature' cannot be changed by 'nurture'. Similarly success might indicate that nurture is more important than any inborn 'inner nature'. However, what Ryan's case illustrates better is the *interaction* between that which might be deemed natural, his 'inner nature', and the external aspects of 'nurture' which the educational environment offers.

Underachievement can be linked to a whole range of factors, many of which are listed above, including class, gender and ethnicity. Social and cultural pressures, for example peer pressure from other boys – what Ryan's mother describes as 'getting in with a bad lot' (Ahmed 2002: 3) – clearly influences the development, or lack of development, of academic skills. Thus it is more useful to look at the ways in which natural and social matters interact, rather than seeing them as separate and distinct; as one or the other having to be dominant. This is sometimes described as the link between the *natural and the social* and offers important insights into wider aspects of social, economic, political and cultural changes. This interrelationship is experienced differently and often unequally, depending on the economic and social context as well as on those appertaining to the natural world.

In the above discussion it is apparent that, whilst it is useful to pick out key aspects that influence experience, for example of inequality, it is also important to explore the ways in which these dimensions relate to each other and connect. For example race and gender operate together to shape experience. This brief discussion of some of the key concepts employed in the analyses of the social sciences illustrates the extent to which interconnections are important in making sense of social relations and social change.

This book takes a range of such connections in order to address some of the different manifestations of change that are taking place in contemporary society. These relationships include that between the natural and the social, which has particular resonance at the present time. Environmental crises and degradation are big issues at the global level and impact upon communities in different ways across the globe. The advances of biotechnology, genetics, new material sciences, telecommunications and information computer technologies (ICT) have developed with stunning rapidity in recent years. New technologies have created new ways of thinking about the links between what is natural and what is social and how the two are combined. These debates are explored more fully in Chapter 2 in the context of identity, for example in the case of reproductive technologies which may challenge traditional ideas of who a person is and who are their parents. These debates highlight the idea of social construction and the role of social factors in effecting change and shaping human societies.

The issue of which factors might be most influential in particular contexts illustrates another tension, that between individual and collective *agency* on the one hand, and social and natural *structures* on the other. To what extent do human beings shape their own world and how far are they subject to factors outside their control, whether natural aspects, either of inner or outer nature, or structures within the societies in which they live? Social structures include some of the concepts identified above, such as class, gender and race and ethnicity as well as the social, political, economic and cultural organization and the institutions of the societies in which we live. The focus upon change with which this book started also requires some exploration of the experience of change through another relationship, that between uncertainty and the difficulties and insecurities of dealing with change, on the one hand, and the new opportunities and diversity which change offers, on the other. Most changes suggest both but the two are differently weighted in different situations and the tension between uncertainty and new opportunities is a crucial aspect of understanding change.

Conclusion

In this chapter I have set out some of the issues which this book will address and have introduced some of the key ideas employed by the social sciences for exploring changing times. Using the example of a personal story about education, I have attempted to draw out some of the different aspects of the narrative which make it social. By unpacking this story we have seen some of the ways in which knowledge is produced within the social sciences and have highlighted the importance of locating personal stories within the wider social context. This illustrates the interrelationship between the personal and the social and between the private and the public.

The concepts briefly introduced in this chapter are those which will inform the discussion in the rest of the book. The approach taken is one that starts with questions, the kind of questions posed within the social sciences in order to unpack what is involved in processes of change and upheaval, as well as presenting a sceptical critique of the extent of change.

Summary

- *Questions* provide the starting point for the investigation. What is going on? What are the implications of this? What else do we need to know?
- *Concepts* provide an organizing framework with categories and concepts covering the key ideas.
- *Debates* present different views and different perspectives which form *theories*.
- *Knowledge* illustrates the ways in which the social sciences inform and relate to policies; social science relates to action and what we do about social issues and is part of societies where knowledge is of prime importance.

The chapters that follow take a key issue concerned with change in contemporary society and explore some of the ways in which knowledge is produced about this issue and the different claims that are made within the social sciences.

Chapter 2 focuses on a particular concept, that of identity, which brings together the interrelationship between the personal and the social. The big issue here, which is of considerable importance in the contemporary world, is the growth of uncertainty about 'who we are' and the attempts that have been made to secure identity. The chapter introduces the concept of identity through exploring some examples covering the areas of place, gender and Internet identities and the impact of ICT on the formation of identities. This chapter addresses the relationship between the public and the private arenas, for example using the idea of electronic communication to look at the different ways in which people present themselves online. 'Cyberspace' may appear to offer a space in which people can communicate without revealing the gendered, raced, able-bodied or disabled bodies that they inhabit in their lives off-line.

The key questions of the chapter are:

- What is identity?
- Are we more uncertain about our identities in the contemporary world and if so how do we try to establish and confirm some certainties?
- Why are social scientists interested in identity?
- How can the social sciences contribute to our understanding of 'who we are'?

Chapter 3 involves an exploration of what is meant by citizenship in the twenty-first century in relation to community and political action. The big issue addresses the changing nature of citizenship and the question of who is excluded and who is included within the category of citizens. The focus is on equality and difference in the construction of citizenship and the role of the state in relation to inclusion and exclusion, as well as the denial of rights and citizenship to those who are dependent on the state.

Key questions include:

- How is citizenship constructed?
- Who is included and who is not and why not?
- How is citizenship changing?

Chapter 4 explores the relationship between consumption and production and the emerging importance of consumption-based identities, for example in terms of the shift away from traditional class-based categorization and the use of lifestyle classifications. The big issue concerns the power relationship between consumption and production and addresses the question of how far it is possible to focus on patterns of consumption and lifestyle as the key sources of social divisions.

Key questions for this chapter are:

- What is the relationship between production and consumption?
- How do they influence each other?
- How much control is exercised by consumers in this process; where does power lie and how does it operate?
- Are we what we buy?
- What is the importance of class in the relationship between production and consumption?

Chapter 5 considers the importance of place in shaping social relations and life chances. It explores the impact of diverse ethnicities, using the UK as an example of a multicultural society, and looks at the tension between racism and a multicultural diversity which could be seen as enriching and beneficial at this historical moment. The big issue is the importance of place in the contemporary world and debates about the question of multiculturalism.

Key questions include:

- What is the importance of place in shaping life chances?
- What do we mean by race and ethnicity; how do we use the terms?
- What is involved in multiculturalism? Is it possible?
- How far is diversity constrained by racism?

Chapter 6 examines some of the key debates about globalization, focusing especially on the tension between those who see the process as positive and beneficial and those who see it as destructive, for example of local culture as well as of the environment. The big issue is about the impact of globalization. How far do the phenomena associated with it have beneficial outcomes or how far are they damaging? Is it a uniform process? There is also debate about the extent to which globalization produces homogeneity. Are we all the same now? Or, on the other hand, are diversity, resistance and creativity still possible in the face of the ubiquity of global capital. The chapter focuses upon discussion of uneven development and the inequality involved in the globalization project.

Key questions include:

- What do we mean by globalization?
- How does it affect different groups and communities; are some more equal than others?
- What are the positive and the negative aspects of globalization?
- Has globalization contributed to the 'risk society'?
- Is it a uniform process?
- What is the scope for resistance and for diversity?

The final chapter reviews the argument and evidence presented in the book and looks at how far we have come. The 'big issues' have been identified and some discussion of what study in the social sciences can contribute to debate has been introduced. The concluding chapter revisits the key debates in the book about the role of the social sciences and reflects upon the ways in which the social sciences can enhance and challenge common-sense understandings of the social, political, economic and cultural world. The conclusion also suggests ways in which an interest in the social sciences might be developed and pursued with some discussion of the concerns of the different social science disciplines and their application, indicating the links between knowledge produced in the social sciences and political action and policies as well as social change. Knowledge produced within the social sciences is part of the social transformations that are taking place. Social science knowledge is deeply implicated in social change, both in responding to material circumstances, for example in economic life, and as part of the knowledge revolution that is an outcome of new technologies, social and cultural trans-formations. So what are these transforming big issues?

Chapter 2

You and me, us and them
Issues of identity

Introduction

One of the key debates within the social sciences which was identified in Chapter 1 was the relationship between the personal and the individual, on the one hand, and the social, on the other. What links are there between individuals and the societies in which they live? How does the one influence the other? Is it possible to distinguish between one and the other? This issue has been addressed within the social sciences through the concept of identity. Identity offers a means of thinking about and of understanding how the personal and the social are connected.

Having an identity is one of the ways in which we fit into the social world and are marked as having distinctive membership of one group rather than another within society. Identity is also a word with which we are familiar in the contemporary world on the global as well as the personal scale. It is quite a fashionable word, for example in the media we may read of 'identity crises', new identities and the need to secure our identities, such as national identities, for instance as British or English or as European. What does it mean to be English at a time when Welsh, Scottish and Irish identities are reclaimed and there is a devolution of power in the UK? Identity is not only in common use as a contemporary buzz word, it has deep and often very powerful meanings. What does it mean to be British, French or German at a time of large-scale migration across the boundaries of nation states, for example by refugees and those seeking asylum from repressive regimes and economic deprivation as well as the movement of skilled labour that is required by global capital. What meanings are attached to the identities of US citizens in the aftermath of September 11 2001? Conflict in the global arena is often described in terms of competing or conflicting identities: Croats, Serbs and Bosnians, Tutsi and Hutu in Rwanda. These conflicts can be between ethnic groups or between explicitly religious groups such as Catholics and Protestants or Muslims and Jews. The assertion of collective identities can lead to conflict and even violent hostilities. The September 11 attacks on Washington and New York were described in the most polarized of terms, as an extreme conflict between 'us' and 'them' which, in some of the political rhetoric, divided the world into the 'free world' and terrorism. These attacks on 9/11, as the occasion has come to be known, were

og, 9/11

significant in making a shift in the classification of identities at times of conflict and war. Identity became a big issue when the identity of the enemy was terrorism, but had no clear identity marked by membership of a nation state, or even a specific territory or ethnic group. The contemporary world offers examples of many such conflicts arising from uncertainties about identities. In other situations they are linked to the movement of peoples across the globe, whether this arises from the need to seek asylum or the demands of new technologies and the labour market.

New technologies also offer challenges to certainties about identity at a personal level. In 2001, a French woman gave birth to a child using the egg of an anonymous donor, which had been fertilized by her brother's sperm. At the same time, the Italian Professor Severino Antinori announced that 200 couples were to participate in an experiment to produce cloned babies. Both events were greeted with considerable anxiety, much of which was centred on the identity of the people so created. The first case showed how reproductive technologies might be used to challenge hitherto securely held certainties about origins and who are the mother and the father of a child. It was further complicated by the suggestion that the technology could permit a child to be born whose father was her or his uncle even though no actual incestuous behaviour was involved. Cloning seems even more troubling for our sense of who we are. Who are you if you are not genetically unique? Such developments illustrate some of the uncertainties with which we are beset in the contemporary world.

People's responses indicate their desires to attain some kind of certainty in the face of these insecurities. In this chapter we are going to look at the relevance of identity in the contemporary world, what we mean by identity, whether there is more uncertainty than in the past and the ways in which people seek to establish and secure their identities, both within a group, as having a collective identity, and as individuals, fitting into the world in which they live.

What do we mean by identity?

Identity involves aligning ourselves with one group of people; saying that we are the same as them, as well as marking ourselves out as different from other groups of people. We can have a collective identity, at the local or even the global level, whether through culture, religion or politics, as well as having an individual identity, as a mother, father or worker. Identity is not only a word used to make sense of 'who we are' on the global arena; it is what links the personal to the social, the 'I' to the 'me'. Identity includes the idea of '*I*', that is the subject of a sentence. When we say 'I' we have some notion of who it is who is speaking and that it is the same person on each occasion who says 'I'. Identity involves how I see myself and how others see me. The social philosopher George Herbert Mead (1934) used this idea to show how the personal and individual was linked to the social in the development of children. Mead argued that we only learn self-awareness through connecting the 'I' to the 'me'. The 'I' is the unsocialized child who is a collection of needs, wants and desires and the 'me' is the social self. Children become autonomous adults who are able to take up different identities and develop self-consciousness, having moved from imitating the actions of others as small children, to understanding how others see them and being able to look at themselves from the outside, ultimately from the perspective of the society in which they live. Through this process the personal and the social combine and interconnect.

As an individual, each of us has a whole range of identities: as a worker, as a parent, daughter or son, as a consumer, as a member of a community and of an ethnic group, as a fan of a football team, or of a particular form of music or entertainment. These are all part of everyday life. We experience a whole range of different identities in our daily interaction with others. The sociologist Erving Goffman (1959) described these different parts which we play, which I have called identities here, as *roles*. Goffman's focus on everyday life is useful in exploring the ways in which people present themselves to others and for exploring the detail of everyday interactions. Taking on an identity may go further than acting out a role. We have personal investment in the identities, which we adopt. For most people, holding on to some sense of 'who we are', and sometimes more particularly 'who I am', is very important. In the contemporary western world this is manifest in different ways; at the personal level people may turn to 'expert' advice to sort out their sense of who they are. This may be through personal counselling or through the pages of magazines and newspapers, with their problem pages and self-help guides. Television, radio and the Internet also provide us with public spaces in which we can identify with the personal crises of other people. Sometimes we can join in through phone-ins or Internet chat rooms or through being an actual participant as on 'reality TV'. We can vote for the eviction of those individuals we dislike from the *Big Brother* household. The coverage of 'reality' TV programmes such as *Big Brother* strongly encourages identification with some individuals alongside the, often extreme, vilification of others. Identities are the common currency of popular television, offering apparent, if superficial and distorted certainties, about 'good' and 'bad'. At the wider level uncertainties about who we are and the need to protect the certainties of one group, can lead to conflict, which can take the form of extreme violence, as has been experienced in the heart of corporate North America and in the tourist resort of Bali in Indonesia, as well as in Bosnia, Chechnya, Palestine and Northern Ireland. Whether we delve deeper into our selves, in search of greater certainty about 'who we are' or take to the streets in bitter conflict to protect our identities, identity is an important feature of the contemporary world. This chapter looks at why identity is such an important matter in contemporary societies and why it is important as a concept within the social sciences. This will involve picking out the key features of identity and of what matters in the formation of identity as well as addressing some of the debates within the social sciences that make identity such a big issue.

Summary

- Identity links the personal to the social.   *'I' to 'me'* self perception
- Identity involves how I see myself and how others see me. society's →
- Each of us has many different identities. mother/daughter/worker etc
- We have collective and individual identities.
- Identity is a key concept in the social sciences and of major importance in our lives.

Who am I?

Before we move into the broader arena of identity, let's start with an exercise that provides a focus on the more immediate question of 'who am I?'

ACTIVITY   Single Mum/Accountant/ English C/Happy / Tall

Stop for a moment and write down five things about yourself; just the first five that come into your head, that say something about you.

COMMENT

You may have done an exercise like this one before. It is quite often used in order to highlight the ways we think about ourselves and to suggest what individuals might think is important about their own identities. There may be several different points that you have made. You may have thought consciously about your identity and described your social position, mother, Scottish, student, made reference to the job which you do, or you may have listed your visible characteristics: tall, thin, black hair, wear glasses. One factor which many people note when they do this exercise is gender. Gender is a bit different from other social features because it is also usually a visible characteristic; like hair colour or height, it is something others are likely to observe when they first meet us. You may well have noted some physical characteristics, that is those which are visible and which relate to your body. Age or disability, are other features you might have noted. These too may be visible features although this is not always the case. People may not always indicate their age in their appearance; disabilities such as deafness are not visible. One of the other social features is race or ethnicity, which is also likely to be something others notice; race and ethnicity are often visible too. Gender and race are important features that are both visible and social. You can observe these features and they are socially significant. Did you include some reference to these two in your list? It is still likely to be the case that people who are white are less likely to have put 'I am white' on their list as a distinguishing feature of themselves. Why is this? Is it because being white is taken for granted as what is normal? It is not even worth mentioning. As Ruth Frankenburg argues 'white people are "raced" just as men are gendered' (1993: 1); that is, gender is not just women's concern and race is not just about black people. However, in the west it is more likely that 'race' is seen to be the concern of people who are black than of people who are white. Your ethnicity may relate to the place you come from or to your national identity, or perhaps to your religion. Many aspects of 'who we are' are not likely to be visible in the ways that gender and 'race' are, for example the job you do and even how wealthy or poor you are – except perhaps at the extremes of affluence or poverty – as well as your religious or political beliefs.

This exercise raises issues about the social categories through which we describe and make sense of ourselves. Firstly, considerable importance is accorded to visible differences between people; how far do we differentiate on the basis of visible features? Difference is an important feature of identity. We share an identity with those who are similar to us and are different from those who take up different identity positions and these differences are represented so that others can understand them. Secondly, it is apparent that these visible features are social, that is they have social implications and the meanings that are attached to them come from the societies in which we live. Some visible features matter more than others and may have social and economic consequences. For example it may not matter very much if you have black or brown hair, but being a woman or a man, being black or white, may have significant consequences for your life chances, even for your earning potential. Some disabilities may be visible and may affect how other people treat you. These visible differences have social implications that are also the result of social, cultural, economic and political practices. The features that are relevant to our identities, indeed those that make up an identity, are the elements that have some social significance. Factors that contribute to our identities are shown in Figure 2.1.

Some aspects of difference are much more relevant to what is called identity than others. You might have noted aspects of your personality; for example as extrovert or introvert or even your mood, happy or depressed. Personality differs from identity in respect of the degree of agency that we exert in adopting particular characteristics. For example there might be some links between my personality and the type of identity positions that I take up. However, whereas I may engage in some activities, such as following football and going to matches every Saturday and shouting loudly, because I am an extrovert sort of person, I follow a particular team because I want to identify with that team and not another. This allegiance may be the outcome of media coverage of a team and its players and what used to be called 'fair weather' support. Manchester United has massive support worldwide as a result of the team's success and the promotion of its image. There may be several other factors in play. I follow the team that represents the community in which I have lived for some time; it may have cultural, political and even religious links with my own community as in the case of supporters of Glasgow Celtic or Glasgow Rangers in Scotland. In these examples, identification with one team or the other reflects deep-seated, long-held and occasionally very oppositional,

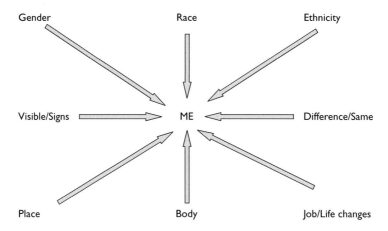

Figure 2.1 Factors that contribute to our identities

conflictual beliefs. What is important is that to identify and take up an identity position there has to be some engagement.

Identification

Having an identity involves being active in some way, even though for many people there is only limited choice. *Identification* is the term often used in psychoanalysis to describe the process of taking up an identity. This process goes much further than just copying the behaviour and attitudes of others. Identification involves taking an identity into yourself. Identity is not only about what others see, for example as behaviour and outward observable expressions of who we are. It is also about the inside, about feelings and the inner space where emotions and desires are played out. Sigmund Freud (1905) used the concept of identification to describe and explain the ways in which children adopted gender identities through this psychological process. One aspect of Freud's account has similarities with that of Mead, although Freud was much more concerned with the problems and conflicts that can occur in the formation of identity than Mead. Freud was also particularly concerned with the impact of the *unconscious* mind on our experience, whereas this is not a concern in Mead's discussion. Freud focused on male children and argued that small boys identify with their fathers, taking in what they perceive to be masculine traits and ultimately a male identity. This process of identification is very powerful and Freud emphasized the importance of early identification with the parent of the child's own sex as forming the basis of gender identity in adult life. Freud's analysis that is particularly important is the extent of the investment that is made in gendered identities (Bocock 1982). The characteristics that are adopted create the person's sense of who they are. Identification may be conscious or unconscious. Freud uses the notion of the *unconscious* to explain the area of the mind into which we deposit repressed feelings and desires. For example, all the times a child's wishes are not met, these unmet desires are repressed into the unconscious mind, from which they may emerge at a later date. They can emerge in dreams or jokes, or in slips of the tongue; those little mistakes that have come to be called Freudian slips. You can probably think of several examples of these. They often involve some sexual innuendo, like the occasions when someone says orgasm instead of organism or sexiest instead of sexist. The Freudian argument is that these slips are more than people having difficulty getting the words out; they represent hidden feelings, which are present in the unconscious mind.

It was suggested in the above section 'Who am I?' that we are recognized and recognize others often by their appearance. Appearance can give some clue as to our identity. Think about it; you might identify with someone who is wearing clothes that signify an identity, such as those that conform to your own religious practice. At sports events we recognize and identify with those who wear our colours or at international events those who carry our national flag and sing appropriate songs. When you are travelling abroad, you recognize as the same those who speak the same language as you. All of these involve visible, or audible, outward signs of an identity. How do we indicate our identities to others? By the clothes we wear, by badges, by signs of belonging such as team colours, logos, designer labels, flags, uniforms, by how we speak, not only language but through accents and regional dialects. All these are signs of belonging to a particular group. It is through these signs or symbols that we represent ourselves to others and come to recognize them. A symbol involves making one object, word or image, stand for another. For example wearing a particular scarf or rosette, shirt or insignia indicates membership of a particular football team. It frequently goes further, by fans wearing a team shirt which carries the name and number of their favourite player. This has become a global currency, especially in the case of some celebrity players. Mead (1934) emphasized the importance of symbolization in the formation of identity and the representation of ourselves to others. We have to be able to think symbolically, using language and visual symbols, in order to imagine ourselves from others' points of view.

Representations

Social scientists have increasingly addressed the question of representational systems in developing understanding of how identities are constructed and how people come to take up particular identity positions. Of course it is not only social scientists who have these concerns. Politicians, commercial enterprises and advertising agencies have employed the insights of social science in developing promotional and marketing strategies which will encourage the voter or the consumer to identify with a lifestyle or image which is being promoted and, most importantly, to sign up for the political party or buy the product in order to do so.

ACTIVITY

Can you think of examples of products that in their advertising invite the consumer to identify with a particular attractive lifestyle, rather than simply extolling the properties of the product? What sort of links are being made?

Cars → lifestyle → Fiat Punto → youth/friendship
Bmw → status / wealth

COMMENT

Car advertising often uses attractive, affluent, well-dressed, young people, to represent a lifestyle. The implication is that if you buy the product you will assume the identity of a good-looking, well-off, thirty something professional. Advertisements promoting food or household products often connote both a desirable lifestyle and caring, successful parenthood, especially motherhood. Much contemporary advertising plays with ambiguities, for example the Calvin Klein images of androgynous young people, where it is difficult to distinguish between those who are female and those who are male. Some companies offer contradictory messages which challenge any simple association between the product and the image presented. The more radical and controversial of these include the Benetton clothing advertisements, which promoted the 'unlimited colors' of Benetton clothing with images as unexpected as those of a person dying of AIDS and a newborn baby, covered in blood. Images deployed in advertising are carefully considered, according to criteria which derive from social science research as well as that of marketing. Meanings are constructed through representations, not all of which are quite so easily readable as the ones I have suggested here. The images presented in Plate 2.1 and Figure 2.2 may require more expert interpretation to 'read' them successfully.

Plate 2.1 and Figure 2.2 are examples of visual images which appear to mark out a person even before that person has been born. What does the visual image tell us? What meanings does it produce? Do such images reveal a 'truth' which can be seen as reflecting something which is real, something which presents a faithful reflection of reality?

This image, of the foetus *in utero*, is one that many parents in many parts of the world cherish as the first true reflection of the baby that the woman is carrying. Whereas, prior to the arrival of foetal ultrasound scanning, the proof that a woman was carrying a child would be through her own experience of the movement of the child in her body, endorsed by the experienced hands of a midwife, 'proof' in the twenty-first century, is visual. The baby would only be seen after delivery. Does the foetus have an identity? Does the mother have an identity? The foetus might be deemed to have an identity having been captured in this visual image. Think about how many occasions there are in the contemporary world when your identity is secured through a visual image. This could be the photograph on an identity card (ID), the passport photograph, driving licence or security card. People often rely on a photograph to confirm that they really are who they say they are, even that they exist at all. In the case of foetal ultrasound imaging the picture is both proof

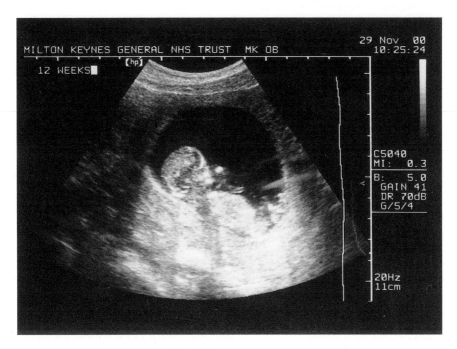

Plate 2.1 Seeing is believing: foetal image

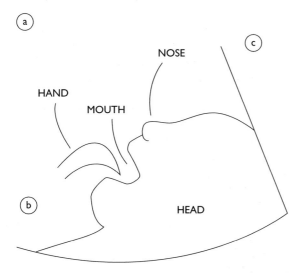

Figure 2.2 The image interpreted

that the foetus exists and that the foetus apparently has a separate identity from the mother. This image of the free-floating foetus gives no indication of its dependent symbiotic status. It is possible to provide an image that is separate, suggesting an independent identity too. This suggestion is exaggerated by the absence of the mother in the image. We know the foetus is entirely dependent and cannot exist without the mother. Rosalind Petchesky (2000) argues that the photographic image as produced through ultrasound scanning, connotes wider social and cultural meanings, that is it produces meanings by association. She argues that photographs are not simple reflections of something real.

Petchesky uses this example to show the privileging of the visual image. If you have a picture of something or of someone then it must be real and that must be 'how it is'. However, it is the technology that makes possible the representation of an embryo inside the womb and the representation of foetus and mother as separate, independent beings.

The specific example, which Petchesky uses, is taken from a US anti-abortion film *The Silent Scream*, which clearly has a particular political position. However, her arguments apply to the privileging of the visual as the primary means of knowledge in western traditions of knowledge. As she says, the visual has a peculiar property for detachment and apparent objectivity by creating a distance between the person who sees and what is seen (2000). She cites her chosen example as relying 'on our predisposition to "see" what it wants us to "see" because of the range of influences that are out of the particular culture and history in which we live. The aura of medical authority, the allure of technology, and the cumulative impact of a decade of foetal images . . . make it credible' (2000: 174).

Visual representation may have a particular place in constructing identities but they are also closely linked to other discursive fields and senses other than the visual. Representations involve the images, words, sounds and practices through which meanings are expressed. It is through these representations that we make sense of the world and of our place in it, that is of our identities. It is little wonder that advertisers are interested in how systems of representation work! The cultural theorist Roland Barthes (1972) argued that what he called texts include all forms of *representation*, not just words and images but ceremonies, rituals, clothes, films, buildings, hairstyles and television programmes. This gives plenty to work with, but new technologies provide additional texts and we could add the Internet as another site for the production of meanings about who we are and who we could be.

In the rest of this chapter we look in more detail at the processes involved in the formation of identity and at the factors which can be included. These involve different dimensions of identity – such as gender, ethnicity, where you come from or where you live, the body and life chances – which are the sort of aspects you might have picked out when describing yourself. All these might suggest aspects of who we are which could provide some stability. In an uncertain and changing world, maybe being a woman or a man, having a particular national identity or religion could offer some security and a basis for establishing our identities. Or do they?

Summary

- Identities are made up of different dimensions which include gender, race, ethnicity, work, life chances, body and place.
- These dimensions link the personal and the social and mark difference and sameness.
- Different identities are represented and may be shown through visible differences and signs.
- Identity involves personal investment through identification.

Who r u?

Text messaging may be cryptic and reveal little of who we are, but it represents a shift in methods of communication and changing times in which the advent of computer technology and the speed of newly developed communication systems may be changing the ways in which we represent ourselves to others. Text messaging goes far beyond sending details of meeting times and dates, or times of arrival. Texting has its own codes and meanings and provides a means of establishing a shared identity with those with whom we communicate.

Home pages provide a means for ordinary people, as well as the rich and famous, to represent themselves in a public space, which is accessible to everyone who is able to log on to the Internet. (You could try this out if you have access, and log on to a site such as WebRing, at www.webring.org.) Home pages are indications of how people seek to present themselves to others. People have to select those aspects of themselves that they want to present to the outside world. This means the aspects of your own identity to which you would like to draw the attention of others and the methods by which you would hope to achieve this. For example if you were creating (or maybe you have already done so) a home page, which pictures, graphics, music and photographs would you use to give some indication of who you are?

Online?

Electronic mail provides a very rapid means of communicating (and allows for much more elaborate text than the messages of the mobile phone, although the style is often just as minimalist) and the Internet offers sites on which we can represent ourselves and adopt a range of different identities.

ACTIVITY

Read this short account of an early example of a computer communication which seems at first to indicate some very positive possibilities for this medium, but which may present some problems about identity online. What is your reaction?

> Rosanne Stone Allucquere describes a computer conference in which a person, whom she calls Julie, participated. 'Julie was a totally disabled older woman, but she could push the keys of a computer with her headstick . . . On the net Julie's disability was invisible and irrelevant . . . Her heart was as big as her greeting, and in the intimate electronic companionship that can develop during on-line conferencing between people who may never physically meet, Julie's women friends shared their deepest troubles, and she offered them advice . . . Julie herself was sharp and perceptive, thoughtful and caring.'
>
> (in Branwyn 2000: 505)

After several years, and a great deal of disclosure, Julie was found to be an able-bodied, middle-aged, male psychiatrist. This proved shocking to those who had been party to intimate exchanges with Julie and the women who had shared the conferences with 'her' were very angry.

COMMENT

Do you find this deception disturbing? The form of deception may be specific to the technology, which no doubt is facilitated by disembodied communication. Nobody could see Julie or her disability or the fact that 'she' was a man. Deception takes place in other communicative media, including those which involve 'real' bodies, although computer technology affords greater potential for anonymity. Allucquere (2000) cites this as an early example of computer cross-dressing or 'passing', which reveals some of the more disturbing aspects of disembodied communication. She suggests that this early example illustrates the disruptive potential of computer communication. Appropriations of the other gender produce new modes of interaction. The ways in which women and men employ what may be relatively stable assumptions about what is appropriate for a female or a male persona in computer communication, may have become more flexible. There are some instances of women 'passing' as men online and gaining confidence in the process although men are more likely both to participate in such online communications and to pass as women than women are as men.

However, the Internet can offer valuable means of communication for people with disabilities. Mike Featherstone (2000) cites examples of people with severe physical disabilities who are able to use their computer to engage in mobility and sensory exploration. By mixing computer technology with the body, people are able to achieve greater freedom in shaping their own identities. Online, people can reconstruct and create their identities. Martin Wroe cites the work of John Suter, professor of psychology at Rider University in the United States, who claims, on his website, that online discussion encourages people to feel free about expressing themselves. Suter claims that textalk is unencumbered by the interferences of face-to-face communication such as gestures, facial expression and appearance. It is because 'cyberspace presents an alternative social reality, participants take on roles they might never dream of in real life . . . a shy person comes to realise the delight of spontaneously opening up, and how that leads to friendships' (in Wroe 2002: 50). These views present very optimistic readings of the opportunities afforded by cyberspace! However, as Wroe notes, online identities are not all positive: 'The peculiar on line cocktail of intimacy and anonymity, immediacy and distance encourages visitors to become abusive much more rapidly than in real life' (2002: 50).

The Internet offers a site for the presentation of sexual identities which can be a valuable resource for those who are sexually marginalized by the society in which they live (Tsang 2000). For example coming out online is an important stage in defining sexual identity. Although computer communication offers a public space for the expression of intimate feelings, the 'real' embodied person may feel more confident in this disembodied space. However, traditional assumptions are made about speaking as a woman or as a man online. Whilst offering a space for the exploration of new sexual identities or the possibility of greater freedom of expression than are experienced off-line, most bulletin board systems where people communicate involve presentations of the self which draw on existing gender roles. They also involve descriptions of real-world circumstances and the establishment of some context that relates to the 'real' world. Some participants use communication on the Web to express their off-line anxieties, using the bulletin board as a kind of counselling service.

People may also enjoy the speed and intimacy of email communication even in situations where they frequently meet the people with whom they are communicating. Young people notoriously run up high bills texting their friends on their mobile phones, even whilst in the same room! The Web may be disembodied but it is still 'real' bodies who press the keys and write the scripts. It is 'real' bodies who live off-line. The 'real body' may belong to a man of 47, who is passing as a youth and communicating with a girl of 13 whilst she enjoys the privacy of her bedroom. The anonymity of virtual reality is only called into question when the 'real man' attempts to meet up with the child of 13, what is euphemistically called 'off-line' (*The Observer* 18 March 2001).

On TV?

The Internet does, however, offer a new, public space in which to explore and reconstruct identities. Increasingly, private feelings and personal identities are presented in such public spaces. People are encouraged to explore and reveal their own feelings in public spaces such as those offered by 'reality TV' for example in programmes such as *Big Brother*, *The Oprah Winfrey Show* and *Jerry Springer* and radio phone-ins, as well as in chat rooms and on bulletin boards on the Web.

The formation of identities can be illustrated through the link between such public and private spheres.

The following example includes two such public spheres, the Internet and a television show and may be illustrative of changing times, for the expression of identities, as well as suggesting some changes to identities which we might have thought were fixed and unchanging. We might have expected the identities of mothers and fathers to be 'natural' and to some extent certain. On 1 February 2001, two married couples appeared on *The Oprah Winfrey Show*. Each couple thought that they had adopted a set of twin girls who had been advertised on the Internet. Arrangements for the adoption had been made through a third party. The mother of the twins had at first wanted to have her babies adopted but later decided she wanted to keep them after all, by which time the biological father, the mother's estranged husband, had also decided he would look after the babies. The television show was described as 'Oprah acts as Solomon in dispute over Internet twins' (*The Guardian* 2 February 2001, p. 6). Firstly, the babies were advertised on the Internet, secondly an extensive media debate followed the claims of two different couples – one in the United States and the other in the United Kingdom – to have adopted the babies and finally the couples were brought together for a media judgement on a popular TV show. What can this tell us about identity? Does this scenario suggest that significant changes have taken place in the formation of a particular identity, namely that of a parent, or more specifically of mothers? Firstly, what could be said to have changed about this identity and secondly, what could have led to such changes taking place?

This is a complex issue and my concern here is not to address the ethical questions. Our questions relate to what this scenario can tell us about identity in the twenty-first century; how far it presents a transformation and if so what form the transformation might take. This scenario certainly involved a great deal of public display, including the Internet, television and other media, of what might be seen as a very private, intimate relationship between mother and baby, parent and child. Adoption is not a new phenomenon, neither is surrogacy, although the Internet provides a new means of making information available. Who is the 'real' mother and who should be allowed to be the mother of these babies? Is maternal identity one which is not only available to those who can physically give birth, but to those who have the resources with which to 'buy' a baby? So public a forum for the debate may suggest a change in the location for the expression of personal feelings and even for the locus of actual decision making. The birth mother did not appear on the Oprah show, although it was stated that she had changed her mind about adoption. The third party 'facilitator' who had arranged the adoptions did not appear either.

The law and legal procedures, however, underpin any discussion about the establishment of parental rights. Maternal identity, like paternity, may now be a legal rather than a biological category. The issue here seems to be about who should be the parents of the children and who has the claim to be the 'good parents'? Parental identities are not 'just' a matter of biology. Being a good or bad parent is very much determined by social values and expectations and material, economic factors. Even an identity that may appear natural is subject to social factors and to public discussion. The form which this public discussion takes has changed though. There may be more to consider than the ways in which identities are expressed and represented, although this example does offer illustration of a changing place for meanings about the parent–child relationship to be expressed and understood. Economic and social circumstances contribute to imbalances of power which also shape personal relationships and the degree of choice that those involved are able to exercise.

Expressions of the personal in public may suggest a new phenomenon. However, there are other ways in which personal relationships and experiences can be seen as changing. As we saw in Chapter 1, there is evidence of changing social trends in patterns of domestic living, of childbearing and rearing and of patterns of sexual relationships, which might imply shifts in personal and private relationships. In the west, high rates of divorce, increased numbers of people cohabiting rather than marrying, increased numbers of children born to unmarried parents or lone mothers and of single-person households, the greater recognition (if reluctant in some societies and not full acceptance in most) of same sex relationships, all point to social change. Not only is it now possible to advertise surrogacy or babies for adoption on the Internet, other aspects of technological development can be seen to transform the mother–child relationship.

High-tech babies

New technologies make even childbearing – the most embodied of human relations, when one body is enclosed within another – seem both disembodied and distanced. Artificial reproductive technologies have created the possibility of a woman carrying a foetus which was produced *in vitro* by the fusion of another woman's egg and the sperm of an anonymous man. The baby, if carried to term, could become the child of yet another, adoptive parent or parents. Who is the child's mother in this situation? Is it the host mother who carries the foetus and gives birth to the baby? Or is it the genetic mother who provided the egg, or the person who puts in the long-term hard work and provides care for the child? In such a scenario the possibilities of technoscience confuse existing understandings of parental identities.

In 2002 a dispute arose about the birth of mixed race twins to a white couple who had undergone fertility treatment and *in vitro* fertilization (IVF). A black couple, who were involved in the same IVF programme, were unsuccessful in having a baby and it seemed that the white woman had given birth to their genetic babies. However, it was subsequently found that the babies were the genetic outcome of the white woman and the black man. An appeal to law was the outcome. As the secretary of the British Association of Adoption and Fostering, Deborah Cullen, said, 'the law is having trouble in keeping up. When the 1984 Warnock inquiry produced its recommendations leading to the 1990 Human Fertilization and Embryology (H.F.E.) Act and the establishing of the H.F.E. Authority, donor conceived children were looked upon very differently and the technologies were nowhere near as advanced as they are today' (in Lee 2002: 3). Now courts are faced with new problems. According to Allan Levy, QC: 'The woman who carries the embryo is in law the mother. If the other couple lay claim to the children, the twins may be made wards of court' (ibid.: 3). Thus new technologies have created new identities, and new categories of person, with whom the legal system has to deal. Before IVF the 'biological' mother would have been the genetic mother as well, and there would have been just two possibilities – the biological and the social mother.

In this instance the case of the woman who gave birth to the children might be stronger because the longer the babies stayed with her, the greater would be the bonds of social mothering. Courts have to pay primary attention to the needs of children and a change of circumstances and of carer could be disadvantageous. However, other factors are taken into account which include 'the child's age, sex, background, any characteristics that the court considers relevant, perhaps including race. An analogy may be drawn with adoption cases, where local authorities have said black children should be with black carers' (Gieve in Lee 2002: 3).

The court decision announced on 26 February 2003 stated that the babies could remain in the care of the birth mother and her partner, called Mr and Mrs A, but that the children's 'legal father' would be their biological father, Mr B. Mrs A is also their 'legal mother'. This decision creates new categories and new complexities, the implications of which are yet to be resolved, for example in terms of what access should be accorded to the children's 'legal father' and whether Mr A could gain legal status by adopting the children. At the time of writing it is still possible that Mr and Mrs B will appeal against the decision (Dyer 2003: 2).

What is at issue here? How have technologies affected our understanding of identity and our attempts to secure it? What is the problem for the courts? This example brings in a whole range of factors which impact upon identity. This case is one which seems to highlight contemporary changes and technological advances and combine biology, technologies and the legal dimensions of identity. However, visible difference as classified by 'race' in the discussion above which is not a new dimension of identity, is of considerable significance here. Would the identities of the twins and the identity of their 'real' mother be at stake if it were not for the recognition of visible difference and the social impact of 'race'? Courts have to acknowledge the impact of race and of ethnicity and belonging on a child's well-being.

Whilst biology might appear to offer some certainty in establishing identity whether in terms of gender or other embodied features, this example makes a simple notion of 'biology' highly problematic. Does biology mean genetic inheritance, in which case security might be offered by the children being brought up by the mother whose genetic imprint they carry. However, 'biology' also involves the processes of gestation, birth and lactation, which, because of IVF, belong to a different woman. Genetic inheritance is also contributed by the father, which raises a further question above the primacy of the mother or the father, again a largely social, and possibly legal, question.

This example illustrates the complexity of identity claims and especially of the difficulty of attempting to claim certainty by appealing to biology. It also shows that it is impossible to disentangle the 'biological' and the social, or the natural and the social. The two are interconnected at every point, and in this case we have to appeal to legal processes as part of the social structure, in order to make sense of who we are. These examples offer illustration of the ways in which personal relationships can be seen to be subject to change, in different ways through social, economic and technological factors and in the relationship between private and public spheres.

Summary

- New communication technologies create new opportunities for presenting and representing identities.
- Virtual identities still draw heavily on the social world which 'real' people inhabit.
- Other technologies, e.g. reproductive technologies create new possibilities and greater uncertainties about securing identities.
- Biological, social, political and legal aspects of identity become linked in our attempts to find out 'who we are'.

Embodied identities

If the body may not offer quite so much security about 'who we are', as common-sense thinking might infer, what alternatives are there for re-conceptualizing the idea that our identities might be rooted in our biology, in the bodies we inhabit? We could reconsider how far changing technologies might constitute new spaces in which negotiations might take place in cyberspace. In the late twentieth century machines made the differences between people and machines ambiguous. Anne Balsamo (2000) argues that virtual reality offers the possibility of constructing realities free from the determination of body-based 'real' identities. Cyberspace is a body-free environment where you can be a woman or a man, no matter which label you carry in other spaces of your life. In MUDs (multi-user domains) or even more dramatically MUSH (multi-user shared hallucinations) people can conduct relationships without ever meeting physically and construct themselves through a whole series of such relationships. How can new technologies open up new ways of thinking about identity?

Cyborg thinking

Donna Haraway, writing in the United States in the mid-1980s, offered the *cyborg* as a concept that challenges traditional constraining opposites, such as natural/social, mind/body, human/machine, human/animal, and breaks down the boundary categorizations. The cyborg offers a new way of thinking about difference and a new way of conceptualizing the relationship between human beings and techno-science, people and machines. Haraway argues that in the late twentieth century there was a breakdown in distinctions between animals and people, between humans and machines and between science and fiction. This can be used to construct the concept of the cyborg, which bridges the gap between human and animal and machine. For Haraway developments in scientific culture have made it impossible to make clear distinctions any more.

> By the late twentieth century . . . the boundary between human and animal, is thoroughly breached . . . Nothing really convincingly settles the separation of human and animal . . . Biology and evolutionary theory over the last two centuries have simultaneously . . . reduced the line between humans and animals to a faint trace re-etched in ideological struggle or professional disputes between life and social sciences . . .
>
> Late twentieth century machines have made thoroughly ambiguous the difference between natural and artificial, mind and body, self-developing and eternally designed, and many other distinctions that used to apply to organisms and machines. Our machines are disturbingly lively, and we ourselves frighteningly inert . . .
>
> The certainty of what counts as nature – a source of insight and a promise of innocence – is undermined, probably fatally.
>
> Machines are quintessentially microelectronic devices: they are everywhere and they are invisible.
>
> (Haraway 2000: 52–3)

Haraway goes on to suggest some new ways of thinking, where the term on the left is replaced by that on the right:

Representation	Simulation
Eugenics	Population control
Hygiene	Stress management
Reproduction	Replication
Scientific management in home, factory	Global factory/electronic cottage
Family/market/factory	Women in the integrated circuit
Family wage	Comparable worth
Public/private	Cyborg citizenship
Nature/culture	Fields of difference
Sex	Genetic engineering

Some of these visions of a brave new world might already be looking a bit out of date, and Haraway might seem to be over-optimistic about what she sees as the future.

However, she is using the idea of the cyborg not only to challenge the division between animals and humans and between humans and machines, but also to confront many such opposites. Marking out one's identity frequently involves establishing the idea of 'us' and 'them'; not just differences but oppositions. So what is the cyborg and how is it manifest? The word is a bit scary and conjures up images of science fiction or of monsters. We are more familiar with cyborgs in science fiction and on the Internet although it is clearly present in the applications of technoscience, for example in reproductive technologies.

Reproduction is an area of human life that might seem to offer the greatest, most essential certainties, yet the advent of reproductive technologies mentioned above subverts even the certainty of motherhood. One woman might provide the uterus and nurture for nine months, another the egg, another the social care once the child is born, one man might provide the sperm and another the social care of the child. Conception may involve two people who never meet, don't even know each other's names and never meet the child or children that ensue.

Within political theory and feminist thinking, Donna Haraway's work, especially her 1985 'A Cyborg Manifesto', is the most famous introduction to the possibilities of the cyborg. She argues that cyborg thinking breaks down traditional barriers. Instead of thinking of human beings and machines as separate and distinct, we would benefit from understanding the combination of the two. Robbie Davis-Floyd (Davis-Floyd and Dumit 1998) takes up Haraway's claim that 'we are all cyborgs now', listing the myriad ways in which body and machine merge, specifically in examples of childbirth, as well as in everyday examples of our use of computers, even wearing glasses and the synthesis of the bodies of those with disabilities with the technoscience which facilitates daily life. She cites the example of Stephen Hawking whose active and important contributions to astrophysics are made possible through human–machine symbiosis. Instead of separating the body, which was equated with failure following illness and impairment, from machine, signifying technological success and outside control, we could benefit from thinking across the boundaries of natural=body=agency, on the one side and machine=culture, on the other. Cyborgs give people control and this merging of body and machine enables us to exercise control and agency. Haraway seeks to avoid the idea that machines are alien and that they necessarily take away our control over our own lives: they are part of us and we are part of them.

ACTIVITY

Can you think of ways in which the idea of the cyborg operates in your own life? Many people wear glasses but it goes further than this! What about those polarizations between what is 'natural' and what is mechanical and by implication 'unnatural'? The machine component can include any technological or scientific intervention.

COMMENT

We have already mentioned some of the ways in which technology and more specifically machines such as computers can facilitate daily life for people with a range of disabilities. New technologies provide ease and speed of communication which liberate people, for example who might be housebound or otherwise constrained. Increasingly, what constitutes the 'natural' is unclear. There are other ways in which some activities and ways of acting are seen as natural! Think of the range of products in the supermarket that purport to be natural. The example of parenting that we discussed above is a rich area for examples of what is natural and what is not. Haraway offers examples on a wider scale that also indicate some of the benefits of cyborg thinking. One relates to infant feeding, another aspect of maternal identity which is distinguished by oppositions of the natural versus the technoscientific and cultural. She illustrates the weakness of an oppositional view, using the example of infant feeding to show the division between 'good mothers' and 'bad mothers' and between natural and technological (unnatural).

Haraway (1997) focuses on infant mortality rates in developing countries and uses the work of Nancy Scheper-Hughes (1992) in Brazil, where breastfeeding declined drastically at the end of the twentieth century. She asks why poor women stop breastfeeding. Rather than thinking through the opposition of either promoting breastfeeding as natural, or improving bottled formula cow's milk to make it more like breast milk, Haraway argues we do not have to take sides. She suggests that breastfeeding is practice and culture, just as technoscience is practice and culture; the body is historical, natural, technical, discursive and material. The cyborg combines all these elements. A cyborg solution is to employ technoscience to advance not only ways of feeding infants but to support mothers, technically, materially and through how they are represented and given voice to provide them with the possibility to choose, to choose to breastfeed their infants even. This illustrates the agency of the cyborg; the choice is not between women on the one hand and technoscience on the other, a combination of the two can embody agency in women as mothers.

Haraway is very optimistic and sees cyborg thinking and cyborgs as making it possible to include women who have been denied rights to mother children, such as post-menopausal women, socially excluded women, minority ethnic women, lesbian women. This can be illustrated through the challenge which cyborg thinking offers to what constitutes the 'natural'. Frequently, in talking about motherhood, the natural is invoked. This often elides with the normal and the morally approved, for instance in access to reproductive technologies, to adoption and access to children, for example after divorce or relationship breakdown or even whose children are taken into care and whose are not. Once the oppositions are broken down it becomes much more difficult to appeal to one side as right and the other as wrong.

The cyborg overcomes the limitations of opposites, such as nature/culture, public/private. The mixture of technology and biology of cyborg thinking suggests all sorts of new possibilities, especially for those who have been dispossessed and excluded, the developing world in relation to the developed world, women in relation to men. In a set of unequal opposites cyborg thinking offers the chance for the powerless to challenge the hierarchy. The cyborg, through its amalgamation of human and machine, presents a unity between body and machine which can be united under one idea of 'I', that is the subject who makes decisions and acts.

However, in spite of Haraway's concern to amalgamate socialist, feminist and technoscientific thinking there are still some uncomfortable questions about the cyborg and its representations. Who has the power to construct the cyborg and to benefit from its challenges? How does this kind of thinking give more choice to people who lack material resources? Whilst cyborg thinking seeks to resolve some of the limitations of the division between the natural and the social and mind and body, it still does not address the material, economic divisions between people. It is also the case that it does not compensate for the constraints of physical impairment, although technological advances can offer considerable help to people with disabilities and present them with more choices. A major contribution of cyborg thinking is its challenge to rigid oppositions and the way it encompasses technological advance to rethink the role of the body in shaping identities. Cyborg thinking might have little impact on material circumstances and in particular on the economic conditions under which identities are forged.

Summary

- Identity is embodied and our sense of who we are is closely tied to the bodies we inhabit.
- Although the body might appear to offer some certainties about identity, the natural and the social, our bodies and the societies in which we live are interrelated and cannot be simply disentangled.
- Social, political, cultural and legal matters are all involved in the production and experience of embodied identity.
- Even cyberspace, where it might seem possible to present a disembodied identity relies on both 'real' bodies and the social and cultural meanings that are attached to them, for example as women, men, black, white and disabled people.
- Cyborg thinking offers one challenge to the idea that there are distinct separations between simple opposites, such as body and machine.

Buying and selling: material identities

Our understanding of who we are and the ways in which we represent ourselves to others are clearly influenced by our material circumstances. These material circumstances include a whole range of social divisions, such as where we live, access to employment and especially our access to financial resources and what can be called our social class position. The contemporary social sciences focus less on class as the social division which is the key determinant of life chances and identity, than was the case in the past. This is discussed in more detail in Chapter 4, but in this section I want to look at some of the arguments about the extent to which identities are shaped and influenced by the interrelated processes of production and consumption and the impact of material circumstances upon identity.

Consuming identity

Can you buy an identity off the peg? Do people know who you are by the clothes you wear and the possessions you display, or maybe more significantly by the possessions you don't display because you don't have them? How important are patterns of consumption in indicating who we are? Pasi Falk (1994) has argued that identity in modern times is increasingly a consuming self. People in the west, most specifically those with some degree of affluence and access to spending power, are familiar with the notion of 'retail therapy' and the idea that when the going gets tough, the tough go shopping. Anthony Giddens has argued that patterns of consumption and lifestyle are increasingly important:

> In modern life the notion of lifestyle takes on a particular significance. The more tradition loses its hold, and the more daily life is reconstituted in terms of the dialectical interplay of the local and the global, the more individuals are forced to negotiate lifestyle choices among a range of options.
>
> (Giddens 1991: 5)

Although Giddens acknowledges the structural factors of *capitalist* production, he underplays its inequalities. The options for many people across the globe and even within affluent western countries are not between lifestyle products but about how they can manage to sustain daily life. It is only possible to construct the self through lifestyle choices and patterns of conspicuous consumption, if one has the resources so to do. Poverty and inequality offer significant counter arguments to the claim that we are what we buy and that consuming identities afford greater agency to those who buy into identity positions through the consumption of goods and services. There are clearly material constraints to some of these arguments. However, the development of consumption theories and the higher profile given to consumption in economic systems in shaping and providing a means of securing and shaping identities is largely intended to counter the underplaying of cultural factors in earlier accounts that prioritized *production* and the economic base of social relations and divisions.

There are, however, other limitations to the claim that we are free to manage lifestyle identities and exercise autonomy in the process through consumption.

How do we make decisions about which lifestyles to buy into? Other approaches to the phenomena implicated in consumption patterns are more aware of the ways in which consumers are constrained, not only through lack of resources. Such views emphasize the influence that corporate *capital* is able to exercise in shaping the decisions that are made by consumers, indicating dependence and lack of autonomy among consumers. We are not simply free agents, floating through the paradise of consumption and fulfilling our desires.

ACTIVITY

Read this extract from Grace Nichols's poem from her collection *The Fat Black Woman's Poems*. Do high street stores offer such choice?

The Fat Black Woman Goes Shopping

Shopping in London winter
Is a drag for the fat black woman
Going from store to store
In search of accommodating clothes
And de weather so cold

Look at the frozen thin mannequins
Fixing her with grin
And de pretty face salesgirls
Exchanging slimming glances
Thinking she don't notice

Lord is aggravating

Nothing soft and bright and billowing
To flow like breezy sunlight
When she walking

The fat black woman curses in Swahili/Yoruba
And nation language under her breathing
All this journeying and journeying

The fat black woman could only conclude
That when it comes to fashion
The choice is lean

Nothing much beyond size 14
(Grace Nichols 1984)

COMMENT

Grace Nichols, with some amusement, sums up some of the contradictions of the free market of choice where identities can apparently be bought off the rails at high street stores. She wistfully dreams of representing herself as she would like to be, but can find no appropriate garments in the stores wherein lie such cornucopias of choice. Markets depend on the creation of desires as well as responding to needs in consumers, and women form a significant part of the market, especially in relation to clothes and cosmetics.

Arlie Hochschild (1994) has suggested that the feminist project of increasing women's independence has been curtailed by the images that consumer cultures – for example as promulgated within the women's magazine market – use to promote the idea of women using purchasing power to please themselves. This view is challenged; there is also space for the exercise of some independence and autonomy within such consumer cultures, for example as in women's magazines (Woodward 1997). Women are not simply the passive recipient of distorted, glamorous lean images. They can enjoy both the images and the aspirations they express and retain some critical awareness.

Zygmunt Bauman argues that social skills have become undermined by an excessive concern with individuality and the consumption that people are compelled to engage in by the market forces of the capitalist economy in late modernity.

> Unable to cope with the challenges and problems arising from their mutual relations men and women turn to marketable goods, services and expert counsel: they need the factory produced tools to imbue their bodies with the socially meaningful 'personalities'' medical or psychiatric advice to heal the wounds left by previous and future defeats, travel services to escape into unfamiliar settings which it is hoped will provide better surroundings for solution of familiar problems, or simply, factory produced noise (literal and metaphorical) to 'suspend' social time and eliminate the need to negotiate social relations.
>
> (Bauman 1987: 164)

Bauman presents a more constraining view of consuming identities than some of the views that express this phenomenon as potentially liberatory and as opening up new, democratic possibilities for forming and representing identities. However, the ironic play on the assumptions and contradictions of consuming identities that has become a part of popular culture in the west, is very much in line with the practices of contemporary capitalism, although consumption can no longer be reduced to a function of the capitalist economy, nor a simple outcome of the production process. As Danny Miller argues, consumption is not merely an act of buying goods, it is 'a fundamental process by which we create identity' (1997: 19). Miller sees the process of consumption as creative. Patterns are multi-faceted and diverse, but the main points of his argument are that what we buy and consume contribute to our sense of who we are and that this process is active and creative. Our identities are made up and are represented by the consumer goods that we buy. Consumption is much more than the response and trigger to production; the circuit of production has to include both representation and identity. This is also an active process and consumption is not passively, or crudely, determined by what is produced and how it is marketed.

Pierre Bourdieu (1984) retains a materialist class-based analysis, but incorporates *taste* as exercised by consumers in line with their class identity. Bourdieu took up the idea of the active process of consumption in his work on the ways in which the consumption of goods constitutes the expression of taste. Display of the goods that we have bought has symbolic significance in demonstrating membership of a particular culture. He suggests that consumption is,

> A stage in the process of communication, that is, an act of deciphering, decoding, which presupposes practical or explicit mastery of a cipher or a code . . . taste classifies the classifier. Social subjects, classified by their classifications, distinguish themselves by the distinctions they make, between the beautiful and the ugly, the distinguished and the vulgar, in which their position in the objective classifications is expressed or betrayed.
>
> (Bourdieu 1984: 2, 6)

Thus identities are organized by their classifications and mark themselves out by the distinctions they make. This is the way in which class differences are constructed through consumption. This critique is heavily dependent on classificatory systems, which might indicate a rigidity in the marking of identity through consumption. Bourdieu argued that, although patterns of consumption are varied and diverse, they are socially structured. In fact his main analysis was of class as the major social division, paying more limited attention to other social divisions, such as ethnicity, generation and even gender gets only limited coverage. Bourdieu retained an economically based analysis of class, which prioritizes the economic structures which determine social relationships and saw class as the main determinant of consumer behaviour which is, in Bourdieu's work, largely formed through the economic structure and the outcome of systems of production and ownership. However, consumption is at the same time material and symbolic. Consumption expresses taste and taste lifestyle and Bourdieu's analysis signifies a shift of focus from production to consumption and onto empirically supported claims that identities are created through the process of consumption.

This process of consumption can also be linked to the body. Falk (1994) provides an analysis of the role of consumption in contemporary life with an account of the ways in which the body is involved in taking up an identity. Falk bases his analysis of consumption on the body. Thus consumption is linked to sensory experience and to pleasure, for example in his exploration of luxury and conspicuous consumption in the production of contemporary identities. These identities are produced through the interrelationship between the promotion of products and advertising which target the consumer and the body on which such promotions become inscribed. Think of the myriad ways in which advertisements play on these notions of pleasure in the body – from chocolate bars to cosmetics to cars.

Whilst Bourdieu retains a strong material base in his analysis, some of the developments within the social sciences have focused more on the discursive and representational systems through which identities are produced. A shift towards greater emphasis on agency and diversity, for example in line with the celebration of diversity, fragmentation and pleasure, may open up possibilities for different identities to be created and acknowledged. However, the shift in emphasis from the dominance of economic systems and production in shaping identities may itself open up spaces which, whilst appearing more free and fluid, are equally constraining.

Summary

- Consumption plays a key part in understanding identity.
- We represent ourselves to others and understand who they are through what we buy and how we look, including the clothes we wear.
- There are different views on the impact of consumption on identity, especially between how far we can make our own choices and how far we are constrained by social factors, such as lack of resources and by the ways in which others, including advertisers, determine what we can consume.

Where do you come from?

Where do you come from? This is often one of the first questions we ask someone when we meet him or her for the first time. Knowing where people come from gives us some idea of who they are. For example when we are away from home, perhaps in another country, some sign that a person comes from our home country or even home town presents a point of recognition and identification and thus an immediate point of contact. Even in a globalized culture (see Chapter 6), when all major world cities feature the labels and insignia of the same companies – McDonald's being not the least of these – we still identify with the place we come from and recognize something in common with those who share links with that place.

ACTIVITY

Think about where you come from. If someone asks you the question 'where do you come from?' what do you say? What meanings does this place have for you?

COMMENT

Your response to the question may vary according to the situation in which the question is asked. When asked abroad you may specify your country of origin or domicile, whereas nearer to home you might specify the town or village or the locality, even the street you live on within a city. There are different meanings attached to living in the countryside or the town, or even in particular parts of a town or city. Having a particular postcode can signify certain things about you, especially in relation to your social standing and even your credit rating!

Did you think of the place where you live? Or the place where you were born, or maybe even where your parents were born? Where we live is the outcome of several different factors. People may move across the globe for a variety of reasons, some of which result from the 'push' factors of their original home being too inhospitable, even dangerous, to the 'pull' factors of a better life, including job opportunities in another country. The twentieth century was described by John Berger (1984) as having migration as its quintessential experience. It may be that the extent of migration in the contemporary world, which is not to claim that migration is in any way a new phenomenon, leads to the desire to achieve some form of stability and certainty about identity through myths of origin or claims to home. People need to be able to say that they belong and belonging is closely linked to place, as we shall see in Chapter 5, especially at times of uncertainty. Identity linked to place also matters at particular historical moments, ranging from the extremes of wartime when we are expected to align ourselves patriotically to our own people, to state occasions and even sporting events when people come together to support their country. It is at these moments that we feel we belong to a place and a nation in particular. Benedict Anderson (1983) calls these moments of shared belonging being part of an 'imagined community'. He argues that, although we may never actually come together physically with the people with whom we share a national identity, there are ritual moments, state funerals, royal weddings and international sporting events like the Football World Cup, when we experience a sense of belonging which is located in relation to the country of which we are part.

Links between identity and place may arise more from the categories into which we are placed by other people than those into which we place ourselves. Identity is about how I see myself and about how others see me. I may see myself as belonging to the place where I was born or I may identify more strongly with the place where I live. Certain aspects of visible difference, as were discussed at the start of this chapter, may lead others to classify me as belonging somewhere different from where I place myself. For example black and Asian people living and born in the UK may still be asked where they come from, and at the response which gives a UK location be asked again where they really come from, as if being white and being British were synonymous. 'Race' and place are also closely intertwined, as we shall see in Chapter 5. The UK is a diverse, ethnically mixed society yet there is still limited recognition of that diversity in some aspects of contemporary life.

It may also be the case that we may feel that the place where we live is relatively temporary and that it does not impact upon our identity. However, our actual place of residence provides significant clues as to who we are to a huge range of agencies, including the state. Citizenship rights, which are discussed more fully in Chapter 3, can depend on residence. For example political and legal rights and the right to receive health care and welfare benefits all depend on residence qualifications. The possession of a passport which specifies the country of which you are a citizen, means much more than access to foreign holidays and can for many people be a matter of life or death. One illustration of the ways in which our identities are defined according to place is provided by recent debates about identity cards.

Many European countries, including France, Germany, Belgium and Spain require their citizens to carry an ID card. In 2002 this was mooted for British citizens. The debate surrounding ID cards in the UK illustrates some of the important dimensions of identity which are linked to place.

ACTIVITY

Read the following short extract from a newspaper editorial, published in 2002 following the British Home Secretary David Blunkett's announcement that he was considering the introduction of ID cards. The editorial goes on to express critical concerns about the scheme under discussion but in this first part sets out what it sees as the issues.

What are the issues here and how might ID cards link to identity? What is the difference between an ID card and an entitlement card?

> Yesterday the country was treated to . . . the introduction in one guise or another, of a national identity card.
>
> This time round, it is being cast as an 'entitlement card'. The suggestion that it would play a significant part in combating terrorism has been quietly dropped. Senior police officers who have reservations about an identity card, have been placated by the home secretary assuring them that there is no plan to make carrying it compulsory.
>
> But it is hard to see how the scheme Mr Blunkett is proposing if it has any substance at all, is anything other than a national identity card in all but name.
>
> Not that yesterday's consultation paper makes it clear. It ranges from a simple plastic card, based on existing driving licences and the planned 'passport card' for EU travel, to sophisticated smart cards using fingerprint or iris recognition technology.
>
> (*Financial Times* 4 July 2002: 16)

COMMENT

There is an interesting shift in the language used to describe what is proposed from the more restrictive, policing idea of an ID card, which might be linked to denying British identity to those who cannot access such a card, who are not British citizens, to an entitlement card which seems much more positive in its focus on what you can have rather than what you cannot. The ghost of terrorism, or more specifically of anti-terrorism, haunts the debate. The government is clearly attempting to find a way of monitoring access to citizenship rights, without appearing to be too constraining, but the proposal seems to lack substance since a voluntary card would be likely to have little impact. Place here is understood as the nation state and what people would be entitled to is the benefits of living in a particular nation state – or more accurately set of nations which make up the British state. At a time of change, when it is not only global corporations which cross the boundaries of nation states but also global terrorism, there are different meanings given to citizenship. These ideas are explored more fully in Chapter 3 on citizenship and Chapter 6 on globalization. Citizenship and the rights it affords is a crucial aspect of identity which illustrates different dimensions of identity, especially in relation to who is included and who is excluded. This is another example of identity being constructed around those who are the same and who share an identity and those who are different. In this case those who are seen as different are excluded from the benefits and advantages of those who are included.

Summary

- Identities are often located in relation to a particular place.
- Places are not only geographical but have social, political, cultural and legal meanings all of which strongly impact upon identity.
- Place can be a factor in different aspects of identity, including national identity.

Conclusion

Changing times mean changing identities and a shift in the importance of identity in the contemporary world. In this chapter we have defined identity as linking the personal and the social; as providing a means for individuals to fit themselves into the society in which they live. Identities can be individual and collective. In both cases, whether individuals make sense of their place in the world as individuals or as part of a group, identity has to involve social factors. Some of us have more scope for choosing our own identities than others. For example economic, material and physical constraints can all cut down our options. Changes in the relationship between individuals and the wider society and between what we think of as natural and social, make identity a useful and important concept for promoting our understanding of both change and continuity. Identity is based on difference; on having the ability to mark oneself out as different from others. This marking of difference is often made possible through visible signs and symbols, from our external physical appearance to the clothes we wear and the flags and symbols we use to identify with a particular national or ethnic identity. In many respects there have been significant changes and a discussion of identity shows the extent to which movement and change as well as economic and technical developments impact upon people's sense of who they are. For example in terms of politics and the definition of national boundaries, culture and ethnicity can take precedence over the nation state in defining identities. The migration of people across the world and the breakup of traditional boundaries through the growth of global culture and economics have led to changes in the ways in which people think about who they are and where they belong. What are the differences between us if we all shop at the same stores and eat the same food, provided by multinational corporations? However, people still seek to hold onto their sense of belonging and to their roots. We need to know where we come from and there is resistance to this blurring of boundaries. Sometimes the resistance is manifest in conflict and hostility, for example in conflict in inner-city areas where uncertainties and inequalities have resulted in racist attacks and racial tension.

Technological change has led to faster and, some might argue, more democratic means of communication, which offer new identity positions that can be taken up. Information technologies certainly offer new ways of communicating that can transcend national boundaries. Technological advances have intervened even before birth and lead to confusion of the relationship between parent and child, casting doubt on who is the mother of a child and of the family to which people might feel they belong. We all have to deal with these uncertainties and it is often only though appealing to social, political, cultural and legal practices that we can come to terms with change. The role of the social sciences is to develop new ways of thinking in order to accommodate and understand change.

Summary

- Identity is an important concept in the contemporary world because it links individuals to the society in which they live.
- Identity is marked by difference – we are the same as those with whom we share an identity and different from those who have other identities.
- Social, political, technological and cultural changes impact on how people see themselves and are seen by others; new identities are formed and new allegiances challenge old certainties.

- There are changes and continuities in the relationship between individuals and the societies in which they live but contemporary societies are often characterized by uncertainty.
- Uncertainties arise from technological advances as well as from migration and cultural and economic changes, which can question traditional certainties, for example those linked to the body and to place, ethnicity and nation, class and gender.

Chapter 3

Citizenship

Who's in and who's out?

Introduction

Citizenship is a big issue, especially at a time of extensive movement of peoples across the world and of social changes within countries. Contemporary interest in citizenship arises from a number of different factors. Social changes which are the result of European integration as well as migration, including the pressure of asylum seekers on welfare, health and education systems, have brought issues of citizenship to the fore. Migration is a major factor in population change. For example projections recorded in *Social Trends* data for the UK predict that net migration will exceed net natural changes (births and deaths) so that by 2011 net migration will account for 70 per cent of population change in the UK (*Social Trends* 2002). Changes to the welfare state, devolution and the social rights of nation states, the advances of technoscience, especially in relation to genetics and to reproductive technologies, addressed in Chapter 2, all challenge traditional ideas about who has citizenship status. Family structures and the nature of paid work and employment patterns have changed and sexual politics and the campaigns of identity politics – such as the women's movement and gay and lesbian rights, multicultural, ethnic minority, the disability and environmentalist movements – have led to demands for recognition of the rights to citizenship of those previously excluded. All this calls for a broader understanding of citizenship and even the requirement that UK schools teach the subject as part of the curriculum from 2002. Changing times have led to new political demands and the need for new theories of citizenship.

Citizenship is a category of inclusion and, by implication, exclusion. The category includes those identified as citizens and accords those people rights as well as placing some obligations upon them. This chapter explores what it means to be a citizen in changing times and, in particular, how theories of citizenship can cope with the changes that are transforming social and political life in the twenty-first century. Citizenship is associated with geographical location. As was argued in Chapter 2, your identity is often secured and established through an association with a place and, especially when it comes to accessing rights and benefits, to the place where you currently live. A permanent address might afford some security of identification and, at the wider level, rights linked to a country of residence might be further proof that you have an identity as a citizen of that country. When you are asked for a means of identification what do you present? Perhaps you offer a driving licence or a student card or some form of bank or credit card? Usually those asking want some proof of your identity, with a name and signature, perhaps a photograph, something exclusive to you as well as some evidence of where you live. A passport, if you have one, can offer specific rights through the security of citizenship, as well as the duties that are expected of a citizen of that state. A passport allows people to travel across national borders and, perhaps more significantly, the lack of a passport denies people access to a country in which they might want to live. It is often the lack of an appropriate passport that receives more media attention in the contemporary world, especially when migration and asylum seeking lead to citizens in European countries such as the UK feeling that 'their space' is being threatened by those who do not have the right to belong and are sometimes called 'illegal immigrants'.

Migration has a long history and has been interpreted, experienced and represented in different ways, ranging from hostility in the country of arrival to a welcome to much needed new workers who can redress skills shortages. Hostility and fear of the 'other' and of outsiders may well have always been a more familiar scenario, however. Indeed, in twenty-first century UK, attitudes towards asylum seekers have frequently been negative. In 2000, the idea of detaining asylum seekers was first mooted by the Conservative opposition, by the shadow home secretary claiming, as reported in *The Observer*, 'that if the Tories win the next election they would lock up all asylum seekers in detention centres' (31 December 2000). Political responses and media coverage of the issues both reflect and create anxieties about the perceived threat of large numbers of people seeking asylum, for example in the UK and other European countries. The popular press plays a significant role in feeding the public imagination about this perceived threat and the scale of the movement of people from one country to another. One UK tabloid, the *Daily Mail*, raised the issue of Lottery funding being directed at assisting people seeking asylum. This was followed by the suggestion that those playing the National Lottery should be enabled to state their preference as to which charity Lottery monies should support. The link between the two issues suggested that support for asylum seekers would not be popular among UK citizens who played the National Lottery. The situation of people seeking asylum and the media coverage of the phenomenon can provide some insights into the different facets of citizenship in the contemporary world. These issues are addressed in all media genre; in the popular press, locally and nationally, as well as on the television, radio and the Internet.

ACTIVITY

Read the following extract from a local newspaper in the UK and think about which aspects of citizenship are included in the coverage presented here.

foreign

Jobs for the /\ *boys*

Illegal immigrants have been working on sandwich production . . . Home Office officials have confirmed two workers were removed from the factory after discovering their applications for asylum in this country had been refused. Members of the 2,000-strong workforce have said that up to 200 foreign refugees can work on one shift at the site . . . [management] alerted immigration officials after finding problems with their two workers' papers and have defended their actions.

The report continues:

Asylum seekers and refugees are being drafted in to make sandwiches . . . leaving local workers outraged. Racial tension at the . . . factory is believed to be high after one foreign worker allegedly attacked another with a knife last week.

Home office officials have confirmed that in an operation with . . . police last Tuesday, they netted two refugees working at the site who had already been refused asylum in Britain.

One worker told the *Guardian* this week that the foreign refugees are often brought on to the site by bus and 'regularly come to blows with each other . . . I would say immigrants make up 40 per cent of the workforce – they turn up at the start of a shift and if they are needed they come in. If they aren't they get turned away.'

Other workers said the refugees did not speak any English and cannot understand the stringent health and safety regulations.

(*Worksop Guardian* 2 August 2002: 1)

COMMENT

In this article there are several different terms used to describe asylum seekers. They are 'illegal refugees', 'immigrants' and 'foreign'. Citizenship is defined in terms of what it is not, that is those who are asylum seekers or 'foreign' are not British citizens. The aspects of citizenship which those quoted here and the article itself highlight are the legal and social dimensions. Citizens are those who have a legal right to be called British citizens as verified by the government through the Home Office and they have a right to engage in paid work. Paid work plays an important part in the construction of insiders and outsiders and in the definition of citizenship status. The implication of this article is that 'illegal immigrants' are gaining access to employment at the expense of 'legal' British citizens. The article goes on to quote the employer as saying that the company is in fact unable to recruit sufficient local people (legitimate British citizens) which is why others not so classified have been employed. What is important for our purposes here is that this raises an issue of considerable social, political and cultural importance at present and it does so through raising crucial issues about citizenship; how it is defined and how it can be explained in the contemporary context. The phenomenon of asylum seeking and many other recent social transformations raise questions, not only about what we mean by citizenship but also about the adequacy of the theories we use to explain current practice.

Summary

- Citizenship is a big issue of contemporary concern especially at times of large-scale migration.
- Media coverage can exaggerate the apparent threat of those who do not have citizenship.
- Citizenship has legal, political, social and cultural implications.
- It concerns inclusion and exclusion.

Who is a citizen? What does citizenship involve?

Citizenship is concerned with one of the most basic questions of any society: who belongs to that society? Citizenship status is usually, and traditionally has been, granted according to one of three criteria:

1   by birth in a particular place
2   by descent, according to blood relationship
3   by naturalization through recourse to law.

Citizenship also confers rights and much of the writing about citizenship has emphasized the issue of entitlement. In the example above about asylum seekers, it is the entitlement to paid employment that goes with citizenship status that is most important. This may also be what is seen as most threatening to British workers who, in the above article, are quoted as expressing anxiety about the possible threat to their own entitlement to paid work posed by 'outsiders'. The right to work in a country in which you have citizenship has been a key component of the entitlements, but there are others. Much of the anxiety about the influx of asylum seekers into the UK has been fuelled by media representation of the pressure this movement of people would place upon the social services and the provision of welfare benefits, housing, health and education.

The following extract outlines the features of citizenship as expressed by one of the most influential thinkers on the subject, T. H. Marshall. He wrote about the historical development of citizenship in Britain through the nineteenth and into the mid-twentieth centuries.

I have divided citizenship into three elements, civil, political and social . . . civil rights came first, and were established in something like their modern form before the First Reform Act in 1832. Political rights came next, and their extension was one of the main features of the nineteenth century, although the principle of universal citizenship was not recognised until 1918. Social rights . . . revival began with the development of public elementary education, but it was not until the twentieth century that they attained to equal partnership with the other two elements of citizenship . . .

Citizenship is a status bestowed on those who are full members of a community. All who possess the status are equal with respect to the rights and duties with which the status is endowed . . .

Citizenship requires . . . a direct sense of community membership based on loyalty to a civilization which is a common possession. It is a loyalty of free men [*sic*] endowed with rights and protected by common law.

(Marshall [1964] 1994: 24–6)

Let's unpack this a bit more. Marshall identified three components of citizenship. The first is civil. What does that include? Civil rights are those that are guaranteed through the legal system, that is through the law courts. The law defends the person and the property of the citizen and provides a means through which individuals can seek to protect themselves, through both criminal and, in the case of individuals, civil law. Civil rights are essential to individual freedoms and cannot be denied by individuals or by the state. As we saw in Chapter 2, the law is invoked to protect and assure the rights of individuals at very early stages in their biographies. With the developments in reproductive technologies which create some uncertainties about the rights of the person, this can be relevant even before birth. Marshall locates civil citizenship as the earliest form of citizenship in modern western societies, involving a move from feudal society where status was based on family and class to an individual, uniform status of citizenship.

Secondly, political citizenship gives us the right to participate in activities involving political power, most obviously and most commonly by voting, although holding political office is another aspect of this participation. The 1832 Reform Act gave British men the right to vote. Women did not achieve comparable status until 1928, by being granted the right to vote at 21. In 1918 only women over 30 years of age were allowed the vote. There is political significance in Marshall's reference to the loyalty of 'free men'. Having the right to a free vote, may be a right that is not universally practised, for example in the UK, but the possession of this right is an essential component of political citizenship. To take the debate into more recent times, for example the turnout at the 1997 general election, which returned the first Labour government led by Tony Blair, was the lowest since 1935. In spite of the attempts of this Labour government to involve more people in an active democracy by creating devolved institutions in Scotland, Wales, Northern Ireland and London, strengthening individuals' rights through the Human Rights Act and abolishing the majority of hereditary peers in the House of Lords, the situation did not improve. In 2001, only 59.1 per cent of people voted in the general election, which returned the second Blair government. This was the lowest level since 1918 (*British Social Attitudes* 2002: 199–200). There are, of course, many other ways of participating in political life at a broader level, using a more inclusive and wide definition of politics and political life. The period covered by these two Labour administrations has seen a range of political protests across a spectrum from anti-globalization protestors at the 2001, G8 Summit in Genoa and in 2002 at the Earth Summit in Johannesburg, to the coalition of farmers and lorry drivers protesting about fuel prices in 2000, the Countryside Alliance marches in 2001 and 2002 and anti-Iraq War in 2003.

Finally, social citizenship is the right to enjoy a reasonable, appropriate standard of living, that is one which is possible through access to education and welfare systems. Social citizenship involves addressing some of the problems of inequality in modern society. Access to welfare systems, such as health, social insurance, unemployment and child benefits and housing redress some of the inequalities which necessarily arise in a society based on a capitalist mode of production. Access to education for all provides the means of securing equal opportunities and possibilities of improvement for those who are otherwise disadvantaged and without the means of advancement. In Marshall's account, in order to enjoy 'full citizenship' the concept needs to include all three of these aspects.

Marshall acknowledged the inequality between people especially in terms of economic inequality, and focused his discussion on social class. As we saw in Chapter 3, class is a very important aspect of social divisions. However, class intersects with other divisions and other differences between people. Marshall's account gives very little acknowledgement of the different experiences of women and men and still less to other aspects of difference, such as ethnicity, race and disability. However, many of the differences which so characterize, for example the contemporary UK, could not have been foreseen by Marshall. Devolution, multiculturalism, changing patterns of family life and women's greater participation in the labour market have all had enormous impact in much more recent years. Class is used in a number of different ways within the social sciences as further discussion of these different approaches will show in Chapter 4. *Class* is used as a structure of social division, a means of distinguishing groups of people according to their social and economic position within the society. Class may be based on the work you do, your resources, your status and social standing or your relationship to the means of production in the given society, for example as an owner of a factory or workplace and an employer of others, or as someone who works for wages. The economic inequality of capitalist societies, based on the pursuit of profit, might, as Marshall argued, be redressed through the rights of social citizenship, for example through equal rights to education and welfare, regardless of class position and financial standing.

Could we apply Marshall's account to the more recent example of asylum seekers? They clearly lack citizenship rights, for example civil, political or social rights. Until granted legal citizenship they do not have the right to vote, to participate fully in political life nor to gain access to all the benefits to which British citizens can claim rights. Their situation also highlights the importance of access to paid work which is not detailed in Marshall's account. Being unable to undertake paid work, or only to do so under 'illegal' circumstances, compounds the inequity of their position and they have little scope for appeal to civil rights as outlined within Marshall's definition. It is difficult to explain their position in terms of class alone since they experience a specific form of inequality, as people who do not 'belong' in the country to which they have fled. However, although class is still a significant factor in relation to the kind of work which asylum seekers may be able to undertake, it is still the case that even highly skilled people are compelled to engage in low-skilled work in this context.

Summary   *T.H. Marshall*

- Citizenship confers rights.
- It is closely linked to place, birth and law.
- Marshall's theory of citizenship stresses civil, political and social rights.
- Marshall acknowledges class differences which citizenship can help redress.
- A focus on equality can overlook important differences such as race and ethnicity, gender and disability, by concentrating only on class.

Weighing up the argument

I have suggested that there might be gaps in Marshall's account of citizenship and that we might pose questions about his definition of citizenship. Before going on to look at other accounts, I would like to consider some strategies for evaluating an account such as Marshall's.

One of the key skills in the social sciences is evaluating theories, weighing up an argument and either supporting its claims or countering them and pointing to their weaknesses. We do something like this in our daily lives in discussions we have with friends, colleagues and family, but the whole process is more formalized and substantial when conducted within the social sciences. Even in our daily exchanges it is rarely enough just to claim something is right because you think it is. You usually have to offer some support in order to stand your ground and win the argument. What kind of criteria do social scientists use to evaluate an argument? Firstly, there needs to be some supporting evidence, or evidence with which to counter the claims of the argument. An assertion without any supporting evidence is likely to be very weak. Secondly, the argument needs to cover all the situations to which it lays claim. If it claims to cover all the people in a category then it cannot be sustained if there are gaps and several examples of people to whom it does not apply; if it is full of exceptions. It is important to pose the question 'What's missing?' when confronted with an argument. What does the argument *not* cover. Thirdly, the argument needs to make sense. The conclusion needs to follow from the first claims or initial premises. Can we apply these criteria to Marshall's argument about citizenship?

How useful is Marshall's account and what weaknesses might there be in his approach? His analysis has been very influential, especially within the discipline of sociology, although there have been many recent critiques which have pointed to problems. Firstly, in relation to evidence, Marshall used historical evidence, largely located within the context of Britain. We might want to suggest that changing times present different forms of evidence, which might challenge the claims of a universal category of citizenship. In a changing world, we need to develop new theories and explanations to cope with the transformations that are taking place. Evidence from a very particular culture and history might not fit every instance. Secondly, is everyone included? Marshall refers to 'men' which has been the custom in the social sciences until fairly recently, where the word 'men' was used to include women. However, Marshall's 'men' do not include women. Women are missed out; they did not get the vote on a par with men until 1928. Women's rights to full citizenship in the past, and in some cases in the present, have also been severely curtailed by their lack of access to paid work and the benefits that can accompany full-time paid work. Nor does Marshall's category of 'men' include differences among men, except for social class differences. Thirdly, we might want to raise questions about the assumptions at the outset that citizenship means the same thing to everyone. Marshall's basic premise is that it means full involvement in the community resulting from equal treatment. If people are not the same at the start, treating them equally, that is the same, may not lead to equal outcomes. There are inequalities other than class that could be included and which might change what is important. Gender is one, women's access to civil rights might be different from men's because of their involvement in child care and more interrupted involvement in the labour market. Disability is another factor that might challenge the universal claims of the initial premise. In order for them to participate fully in social and political life there needs to be recognition of the specific needs of people with disabilities and some understanding of difference, especially in the ways in which social organization and the physical structure, for example of the workplace, can operate against full participation. Ethnicity might also be a factor that brings in other aspects of difference not embraced by Marshall's theory of citizenship, which suggests a homogenous society to start with. Failure to recognize the different cultural practices of different groups of people can lead to exclusion from political and social life.

Summary

There are three questions we can usefully pose in order to weigh up an argument. We will come back to these questions when we have looked at some different accounts of citizenship.

- What is the evidence which supports the claim being made?
- Does the claim cover all the situations and people involved or are there circumstances and people left out?
- Do the conclusions follow from the initial premises and does it make sense?

The challenge of other arguments

Another useful strategy for weighing up the strengths and weaknesses of an argument is to compare one argument with another, different approach. Whilst Marshall's approach to citizenship stresses equal treatment of all concerned, other critiques stress the importance of difference. What are the sources of difference and diversity in contemporary society? How might these differences lead to the demand for different treatment in particular instances or is it more just and fair to treat everyone the same? In order to recognize the diversity of contemporary societies like the UK we need to accommodate *difference* among UK citizens as well as demanding *equal treatment*. Some critiques even go so far as to suggest that equal treatment, that is treating everybody the same, may ultimately lead to an increase in disadvantage and social exclusion.

Equality of difference: race and ethnicity

CIVIL — Legal
POLITICAL — vote/repres
SOCIAL — ed/welfare

ACTIVITY

Read this extract from Bhikhu Parekh's *Rethinking Multi Culturalism: Cultural Diversity and Political Theory* (2000b).
What do these examples tell us about equal rights of citizenship?

> In multicultural societies dress often becomes a site of the most heated and intransigent struggles. As a condensed and visible symbol of cultural identity it matters much to the individuals involved, but also for that very reason it arouses all manner of conscious and unconscious fears and resentments within wider society. It would not be too rash to suggest that acceptance of the diversity of dress in a multicultural society is a good indicator of whether or not the latter is at ease with itself.

In 1972, British Parliament passed a law empowering the Minister of Transport to require motor-cyclists to wear crash-helmets. When the Minister did so, Sikhs campaigned against it. One of them kept breaking the law and was fined twenty times between 1973 and 1976 for refusing to wear a crash-helmet. Sikh spokesmen argued that the turban was just as safe, and that if they could fight for the British in two world wars without anyone considering their turbans unsafe, they could surely ride a motor-cycle. The law was amended in 1976 and exempted them from wearing crash-helmets.

(Parekh 2000b: 243)

The Construction (Head Protection) Regulation 1989 requires everyone who works on a construction site to wear a safety helmet, the Employment Act 1989 exempts turban-wearing Sikhs. The 1989 Act considers that the turban offers adequate though not exactly the same protection as the helmet, and is thus an acceptable substitute for it. This means that if a turbaned Sikh were to be injured whilst working on a construction site due to another person's negligence, he would be entitled to claim damages for only such injuries which he would have sustained if he had been wearing a safety helmet. Parekh goes on to cite another example with economic significance.

Many Asian women's refusal to wear uniforms in hospitals, stores and schools has led to much litigation and contradictory judgements in Britain. A Sikh woman, on qualifying as a nurse, intended to wear her traditional dress of a long shirt (*quemiz*) over baggy trousers (*shalwar*) rather than the required uniform, was refused admission on a nursing course by her Health Authority.

(Parekh 2000b: 246)

Parekh goes on to explain that the Industrial Tribunal agreed with the woman's complaint because her dress was a cultural requirement and wearing traditional clothes did not prevent her from carrying out her duties. The Industrial Tribunal decided that asking her to replace it with a uniform was unjustified. However this Tribunal was overruled by the Employment Appeal Tribunal, which took the opposite and much criticized view. However, because rules about nurses' uniforms are laid down by the General Nursing Council, the council was able to intervene and decided upon more flexible rules. This meant that the Health Authority was able to offer the Sikh woman a place on the course with the agreement that as a qualified nurse her trousers should be grey and the shirt white.

GOT TO LOOK AT THE GOAL!
* Here legal reg. did not consider all citizen's. Following letter of law went against cultural requirements.
All inclusive or sufficient flexibility within law needs to be there at outset.
BUT political pressure/time/cost in contradiction

COMMENT

These examples raise some important questions about the rights of citizenship. Are citizens entitled to be treated equally? What if equal treatment leads ultimately to exclusion and inequality? In these examples about dress and the cultural and religious demands of some groups of UK citizens, Parekh is suggesting that we can achieve a more equitable and fairer outcome by recognizing difference and treating people differently. Parekh argues that in a multicultural society, when cultural differences are taken into account, equal treatment is likely to involve different treatment. Sometimes it may even be necessary to those who have been marginalized or ostracized by mainstream culture. The extent of the accommodation of multicultural needs is, however, highly contentious. How far is it necessary to go in extending additional rights to marginalized groups in order to promote greater inclusion and ethnic diversity? Parekh takes a reasoned middle way by arguing for the promotion of cultural diversity whilst accepting that the ability of any society to treat all citizens equally is necessarily limited. He goes on to cite the use of minority languages which can never be accorded equal status with the dominant language, English in the UK. Similarly, he considers the status of holy days and suggests that whilst the common acceptance of Sunday in most western societies puts Muslims, and one could suggest Jewish people, at a disadvantage as they have Friday and Saturday respectively as their holy days, it is unlikely that there will be a complete social and cultural restructuring to accommodate diversity.

The exclusion from full citizenship rights that can result from equal treatment, which fails to accommodate different needs, is not the only important feature of a citizenship that assures sameness. British society, for example, has not only failed to come to terms with cultural diversity in every case, it is also a society in which racism can be part of everyday experience. The Macpherson Report, discussed in Chapter 5, concluded that the racial violence which led to the death of Stephen Lawrence was indicative of a much wider experience of 'institutionalized racism'. This institutionalized racism is a measure of the failure of citizenship in its civil, political and social dimensions. However, although Sir William Macpherson's report stresses the existence of exclusionary practices in major British institutions, it also recommends more inclusive procedures, may of which have since been adopted in an attempt to instate a more inclusive citizenship that addresses multiculturalism. Ethnicity and racialization cannot be examined separately from the other dimensions of difference in relation to citizenship. For example different cultural practices relating to dress are experienced in specific ways for women and for men and may have particular, gendered meaning. Similarly, cultural practices relating to family and marriage also illustrate the ways in which gender and ethnicity cannot be separated when looking at how citizenship rights are experienced.

Individ. citizens need to challenge where society is effectively "letting them down"?

→ By recog diff

Summary

- Approaches to citizenship which assume cultural sameness and stress equality can marginalize ethnic differences and lead to unequal outcomes.
- Ethnicity is an important dimension of citizenship in ensuring full participation.
- A focus on ethnicity must include race and racism as factors which directly counter equal citizenship status.
- Ethnicity interrelates with other aspects of difference, including class and gender.

Equality of difference: gender and sexuality

Many accounts of citizenship have focused on the rights of men. In some instances the word 'men' has been taken to include women, as if there were no significant differences between women and men; we are all human beings. However, admirable though this emphasis on our common humanity may be, it is often men's humanity at the expense of women's, and the norm of citizenship is male. At particular times and in particular societies, 'man' does mean 'man' and women are denied equal rights, such as the right to vote and participate fully in social life and even rights over their own bodies and reproductive rights. The exclusion of women from the rights of citizenship has a long history and has taken different forms. At its most extreme it has meant not only exclusion from political life, through voting and taking public office, but also lack of rights over their own bodies, for example reproductive rights, and over choice of sexual partners, lack of property rights, the right to take paid employment or over choice of where to live and freedom of movement in the public sphere. In the twentieth century, although women had been granted civil and political rights in most western countries, there were still areas of exclusion, notably in accessing the social rights, for example through welfare benefits, which had been instituted to redress social inequalities.

Feminist social scientists have argued that the notion of equality that informs much understanding of citizenship and even campaigns to promote equal rights (like the suffrage movement which argued for equal rights for women on a par with men) is based on an assumption that 'equality' is gender neutral. Carol Pateman (1988) argues that the modern state, far from being gender neutral, is patriarchal. The citizenship constructed and promoted on the basis of notions of equality is thus specific to the interests more of men than of women. Pateman suggests that the modern welfare state, rather than promoting equality between women and men, constructs them differently because of women's association with the family and the private sphere of the home and domestic, unpaid caring work. The different roles of women and men undermine notions of equality and citizenship.

A particular aspect of the different dimensions of gendered citizenship is the changing relationship between public and private arenas, and the experience of intimate relations. The private sphere of human activity and experience has particular impact upon the gendered aspects of citizenship. The private arena of the home and of domestic life has often been taken for granted as associated with women. Relationships with children and with family members and partners may be seen as taking place within the private space of the home and this has also led to women's exclusion from the more public sphere. The public arena of civil and political life and of paid work has been seen as separate and distinct from the private arena of the home. Feminist critiques (Eisenstein 1981; Nicholson 1992) have shown how this distinction has been used to exclude women from the public world of paid work or active participation in political, social and cultural life, or, to marginalize the contribution of women's caring and domestic labour in relation to the wider economy. Nicholson (1992) has pointed to the importance of exploring the public/private dualism as separations which obscure the changing dynamics of gender relations.

Feminist critiques arising from the women's liberation movement of the 1970s focused their analyses on the identification of women as wives and mothers and of the classification of sex, personal relationships and family life as private matters (Eisenstein 1981). Eisenstein notes the history of this separation as deriving from the classical Athenian construction of the male citizen, occupying the public arena of the marketplace and the gymnasium and the relegation of women to unacknowledged domestic labours in the household (1981: 22). It has certainly been the case that women have engaged in economically productive labour outside the household, whether in agricultural labour or, for example, in factory production through the nineteenth century, but this work has been denied or obscured through the higher status awarded to male engagement with public life (Rothman 1992: 128). The marginalization of 'women's work', and indeed of women's lives, as confined to the private sphere has been noted in the classic social science texts.

Janet Woolf has argued that the presence of women in texts produced in the social sciences only existed in relation to men and in the family:

> The literature of modernity ignores the private sphere, and to that extent is silent on the subject of women's primary domain . . . the public could only be constituted as a particular set of institutions and practices on the basis of the removal of other areas of social life to the invisible arena of the private.
>
> (Woolf 1985: 44)

If the literature of the past was silent, that of the present is exceedingly noisy, especially in the discussion of sexuality and, in popular culture, in revelations about the disclosure of the private and the personal in the most public of arenas, especially in the television and radio media.

The argument that sets up the public and the private as opposite and separate is flawed for two reasons. Firstly, it is impossible to separate these two spheres of experience. Life in the domestic, private arena of the home is influenced and structured by social and political activities and policies which are associated with the public arena of the state and of civil life. The experience of individual households and the relationships between the people who live in them cannot be separated from the economic activities of those people and the economic organization of the wider society in which they live. Secondly, it is not possible to disassociate these areas of human experience so that the private arena of the home and of the emotional and personal life are seen as distinctive aspects of people's lives which are not carried into their experiences of the public arena, for example of paid work.

However, the purpose of this discussion of the interrelationship between the public and the private aims to indicate the need to deconstruct some of the assumptions of the separation of spheres in order to explore the impact of the separation on the experience of citizenship.

The social and economic organization of societies also impacts on the personal relationships which people experience, and individuals carry their own experience of the private arena – with the diversities and inequalities which may be manifest there – into the public arena of economic, social, political and cultural life.

Welfare provision has been largely based on the importance of maintaining the family as an economic unit. The views of William Beveridge, the architect of the British Welfare State, established after the Second World War in the 1940s, were that 'the great majority of married women must be regarded as occupied on work which is vital though unpaid, without which their husbands could not do their paid work and without which the nation could not continue' (Beveridge 1942: 49).

Whilst women's 'special role' in supporting the family and male workers in paid employment might have been acknowledged by Beveridge, the full implications of their dependency on male breadwinners was not. Elizabeth Wilson (1977) argued in the 1970s that the British post-war Welfare State was itself dependent on women's unpaid work linking the public and private arenas. Many foods and services previously provided by the family in the private arena have since transferred to the public arena. Wilson argued that it became women's responsibility to ensure that the clients of the Welfare State received those benefits. However, women were not always able to access benefits themselves. For example unemployment benefit, sickness benefit and even retirement pensions are all dependent on the contributions made when in paid work. Women, because of their unpaid caring work have often been unable to qualify for the full rights of social citizenship because of the assumptions made by Beveridge that inequalities could be addressed by supporting men through the welfare system. As Carol Pateman (1988) argues, exclusion from the labour market prevents individuals from accessing the resources necessary to play a full part in civil society. Women's greater participation in the labour market at the end of the twentieth and into the twenty-first centuries has had a significant impact on their inclusion as citizens.

Although there have been significant changes – for example in legislation in response to changes in the workplace, with more women doing paid work, changes in the family with more divorces and lone parents and the growth of multiculturalism

– a legacy of traditional thinking about gender and ethnicity still informs our understanding of citizenship. Diane Richardson (2000) argues that gender has been neglected in the analysis of the national development of the entitlement and obligations of citizenship. She argues that citizenship status is closely linked to heterosexual as well as male privilege, whereby the 'normal' citizen is male and heterosexual. Richardson goes on to suggest that by this standard lesbians and gay men are only 'partial' citizens. For example same sex relationships rarely benefit from the same entitlements, in terms of recognition, pension, inheritance and tax rights, as those of heterosexual couples. Richardson points out that although not all heterosexuals are privileged, for example young single mothers are not, overall it is the middle-class, nuclear, heterosexual family that is 'held up as the model of good citizenship' (2000: 80). Focusing on the example of reproduction, she suggests that what she calls 'sexual citizenship' has two aspects. Firstly, it removes the right of people to choose and to control the conditions under which they have children – or don't. This includes the right to terminate a pregnancy as a sexual right. Secondly, people have the right to choose their own, legitimate sexual partners and experience intimacy, within the given legal framework. This would, of course, include same sex relationships between adults. Sexual citizenship concerns the rights of women in particular to reproduce and to have equal access, with men, in the public sphere, that is to active political and economic lives. Throughout the twentieth century women fought to achieve equal pay, welfare benefits for children and working women as well as the right to vote. To these are added rights related to reproduction for women and to self-determination in areas of sexuality for women and men in order to attain full citizenship status.

Summary

In this section we have seen that:

- An emphasis on equality can obscure differences and lead to unequal outcomes.
- Gender differences impact upon citizenship; women have been excluded both explicitly and implicitly from full citizenship and rights.
- A focus on sexual citizenship includes differences of gender and sexuality.
- The separation of the public and private arenas has been linked to particular understandings of gender.
- The interrelationship between public and private arenas has changed over time.
- These changes and the connections between public and private are well illustrated in relation to citizenship.

Equality of difference: generation and disability

The gendered body is an important dimension of citizenship. Many of the entitlements to citizenship have assumed an able-bodied man, capable of undertaking paid work, as the embodiment of the citizen. As many of the arguments about women's exclusion from full citizenship rights have shown, the marginalization of differences can lead to inequality and exclusion. The importance of paid work in accessing other entitlements, including sick pay, unemployment benefits and, of particular importance at a time of an increasingly ageing population, pension rights, has particular implications for women and for other groups of people who may not be able to enjoy an uninterrupted pattern of full-time paid employment.

Generation presents a significant issue at a time when, for example in the UK the population aged over 60 exceeds that under 16, as revealed by the 2001 UK census. First results of the census indicated that over sixties made up 21 per cent of the UK population, whilst under sixteens made up only 20 per cent (in Carvel 2002). This evidence of an increasingly ageing population which includes not only higher numbers of people aged 85 and over, as well as the over sixties, has led to the expression of anxiety about the financing of pensions and health and welfare support for people of pensionable age. Concern about finance and in particular about pensions has had strong impact at the start of the twenty-first century with turmoil in global markets and falling stock market prices. The near collapse of investments and of European insurance companies such as Equitable Life led to striking reductions in policy payouts and to the abandonment of final salary pension schemes by many companies. Whilst most of the anxieties have been expressed in terms of economic factors, there are significant repercussions on the full participation of retired people in social and civil life. Charities have drawn attention to the likely outcome of demographic changes in a climate of financial and economic uncertainty and flux. They have suggested that 'the changing age profile required a rethink from politicians about issues such as health and pensions, public transport, and ageism at work' (Carvel 2002: 4). Gordon Lishman, Director General of Age Concern England, responded to the first report of the 2001 UK census by claiming that it 'will only be a crisis if we don't address the issues now and come up with imaginative, flexible policies' (ibid.: 4).

As a result of the centrality of employment in industrialized market economies the notion of retirement from paid work has created the idea of dependency in old age. What do changing economic and demographic changes mean for citizenship? Many social scientists prefer to use the term 'life course' for the biographies of individuals. 'Life cycle' might suggest fixed points, whereas life course is preferable in order to accommodate different responses to life events, like getting a job, having children, falling sick, changing jobs and retiring. Different age groups of adults will experience these events within differing social, cultural and economic circumstances, sometimes of constraint and sometimes of opportunity. Thus life course links the individual to the society. Changes in the life course, especially the dependency of old age, have been recognized within the development of the social rights of citizenship. Whilst generation impacts upon citizenship at earlier stages, for example in youth, with demands for legislation to accord young people civil and political rights, to vote, to marry and to take responsibility for their own lives, older generations have assumed more dominance on the political and economic agenda in recent years in some respects, notably in the context of financial support. The primacy of engagement in paid work in order to contribute to insurance schemes and pension funds has led to the exclusion of married women in particular. Some married women in the UK were denied pensions because, although they had undertaken paid work they had only contributed a reduced payment (the 'married women's stamp'). Thus married women were dependent on men – their husbands for support in retirement. Entitlements to pensions are dependent on 'lifecourse interdependencies of child-care and rearing, labour market participation and unemployment' (Twine 1994: 43). Not only is age itself an aspect of difference that has to be addressed in relation to citizenship, generation itself is subject to differences, of gender, class, health and disability. Those who have been least able to make contributions and who have earned low wages through their working lives are also those who suffer most in retirement.

Proposals for dealing with the apparent crises of financing pensions for a growing elderly population at a time of falling markets have to address these differences among that population. Remaining in paid work until the age of 70 assumes people are already in paid work until they are fit and healthy enough to continue. Fred Twine argues that, although retirement occurs at a relatively fixed point in a person's life, the 'welfare prospects for the retirement years are largely set by the interaction of the three elements of citizenship prior to retirement' (ibid.: 42). These three elements include the relationship between the individual, the government and the society, expressed through Marshall's social rights of citizenship. Twine argues that a focus on the life course aspects of interdependence permits connections between reproduction, work and retirement (1994), at a time when global networks transcend the boundaries of nation states and world markets impact upon traditional means of financing pensions and supporting those in retirement. What may appear to be individual experience, located within our own personal body and biography, through ageing, can be seen as linking social, economic and cultural factors operating within a transnational context.

Just as generation and gender have social aspects that impact upon full participation in citizenship so does being able-bodied or disabled influence the experience of citizenship. Disability is another dimension that can be overlooked by the assumption that the rights of citizenship are equal, thus involving equal treatment for all.

Different models of explanation present arguments about appropriate strategies for addressing the problem of the exclusion of disabled people from full citizenship. Strategies for promoting wide inclusion, for example as put forward by the disability movement and those engaged in identity politics and political campaigns, focus on positive action and the limitations of liberal notions of equality. Equal rights have not, on the whole, led to equal participation for women, for minority ethnic people or for people with disabilities. People with disabilities have had to take action to challenge assumptions, especially those of able-bodied people who may have assumed that they know what disabled people want and need. As Lina Abu-Habib argues:

> There is a sense among the able-bodied that disabled people need their protection. Concern with the welfare of disabled people is seen as 'charitable' . . . Achievements and successes in advocacy work on disability can be attributed in large measure to the efforts and perseverance of groups of disabled people.
>
> (Abu-Habib 2002: 266)

One of the ways in which it has been difficult for people with disabilities to organize to express their own needs has been the way in which disability has been constructed as an individual problem. The medical model of disability defines disability as a medical condition which might be treated to permit the individual to 'fit into' what is seen as 'normal life'. Thus the source of authority on disability was the medical profession. This model was challenged by the social model, which shifted the emphasis from the disabled person to the disabling society. Advocates of the social model recommended the full integration of people with disabilities into mainstream society. Political activists and campaigners in the disability movements of the 1960s and 1970s focused on the need to integrate into the mainstream and for the wider society to change and to recognize the needs of people with disabilities.

Whilst there are considerable problems with approaches which see disability as individual and medical, the social model has been criticized for failing to accommodate the diversity of forms of impairment and disability (Goodley and Rapley 2002). More recently, the argument has shifted towards fuller recognition of the different experiences of people with disabilities, whilst accepting the importance of the social construction of differences. The kind of access to public spaces and employment, which women have begun to achieve, has only recently been accorded to people with disabilities through legislation, for example through anti-discrimination laws, such as the UK Disability Discrimination Act and the US Americans with Disabilities Act. In spite of legislation changes disability is still seen:

> as a bodily inadequacy or catastrophe to be compensated for with pity or good will, rather than accommodated by systematic changes based on civil rights . . . disability . . . arises from the interaction of physical differences with an environment . . . the particular . . . disabled body demands accommodation and recognition. In other words, the physical differences of using a wheelchair or being deaf, should be claimed, but not cast as lack.
>
> (Thomson 2002: 234)

Not only does the specific experience of disability impact upon people's participation in citizenship, but also some of the negative social stigmatization of particular disabilities prevents full engagement. For example in the case of psychiatric illness, the medical model may persist and individuals may remain stigmatized by records of illness earlier in their own lives. Anne Wilson and Peter Beresford cite the example of a woman who visited her doctor (general practitioner or GP) with migraine symptoms. Thirty-two years earlier, as an 18-year-old, the woman had been diagnosed as having schizophrenia. The woman describes a visit to her GP:

> As I took my prescription from her outstretched hands, and smiled my thanks, she looked down at my medical card and said in a rather interested voice, 'I see it says here that you had schizophrenia when you were eighteen' . . . In a thin voice I heard myself say, 'That was a mistaken diagnosis. I am absolutely horrified to find it's still on my medical record.'
>
> (in Wilson and Beresford 2002: 149)

Having a 'psychiatric record' can have all sorts of negative effects in different areas of our lives in relation to employment, applying for life insurance, travelling or applying to be a foster parent or childminder (ibid.: 149).

Summary

- Generation and disability also present important aspects of difference.
- Assumptions about equality and equal treatment can lead to unequal outcomes in terms of the needs of different people, according to gender, ethnicity, generation and disability.
- Differences of age and disability have often been reduced to the problems of the individual or to physical differences which obscure the importance of social meanings.
- Social, individual and physical differences interrelate in the experiences of people in relation to gender, ethnicity, generation and disability.

Taking action

Each of the areas which has been identified in the above section as restricting access to participation in full, active citizenship, has also been involved as the focus for action, that is for campaigns and political movements that have sought to effect changes. The new social movements of the late 1960s and 1970s were based around the unequal power relations of gender, race, sexuality and disability. These movements strove to erode the boundary between the public and the private arenas of social life and, in the words of the women's movement, to make the case that 'the personal is political' (Woodward 1997a). These movements and the identity politics which developed from them were not always specifically addressed to the issue of citizenship, but they sought to transform politics to promote greater recognition of those who had been excluded and ignored, for example in dominant and taken-for-granted assumptions about the 'normal' citizen. New social movements challenged the role of traditional political parties and class allegiances and appealed to the particular identities of their supporters, for example feminism appealed to women and the black civil rights movement appealed to black people. 'Identity politics involve claiming one's identity as a member of an oppressed or marginalized group as a political point of departure . . . Such politics involve celebration of a group's uniqueness as well as analysis of its particular oppression' (ibid.: 24).

Identity politics are concerned with both challenging the divide between public and private spheres (see Chapter 2 for a fuller discussion) and with making differences between groups of people visible. The new social movements of the 1970s drew attention to the exclusion from politics and from representation in the public arena of women, black people, people with disabilities and gay and lesbian people. This was achieved through making visible past and current ways in which these people are oppressed and to create new political identities. Putting into the public arena and making visible past and present sources of disadvantage and the power relations which had produced these exclusions, helped to create new identities which brought individuals into public view. Thus, new connections were forged between public and private spheres through collective action. In this sense the public spheres mean the places where decisions are made, and collective action ensured that those who had been marginalized or ignored were not only noticed, but legislative and social changes were made as a result of such action.

New social movements have developed across traditional boundaries of class and party politics, even across nation states (as is argued in the context of the 'information society' in Chapter 6 on globalization), but they also impact upon nation states, especially in terms of political change. Some of the transnational networks of new social movements have been particularly manifest in the activities of environmentalist movements but also have a place in all the areas of concern of such organizations. Manuel Castells has made significant claims for the ways in which new social organizations have combined with new technologies to transform political action:

> dominant functions and processes in the information age are increasingly organized around networks. Networks constitute the new social morphology of our societies and the diffusion of networking logic substantially modifies the operation and outcomes in the process of production, experience, power and culture. While the networking form of social organization has existed in other times and spaces, the new information technology paradigm provides the basis for its pervasive expansion throughout the entire social structure.
>
> (Castells 1996: 469)

The movements for social change and for broader inclusion in social participation and in all aspects of citizenship and civil life are seen as part of a wider transformation which has effected large-scale changes on political and social life across the globe. Whilst these movements can be seen as part of a global transformation of politics, they are also indications of the effects of human agency. They may be new groupings and, in many instances, employ new technologies, but they also illustrate another key concern within the social sciences, namely the relationship between structures and human agency. Through collective action some social structures have been transformed. For example the campaigns of the women's movement have led to legislative change in the passing of laws against sex discrimination and the promotion of equal pay. Similarly the disability movement has achieved some success in the implementation of equal opportunities and anti-discriminatory practices through changes in the law. Thus some social structures have become transformed and reformed as a result of human political activity.

Agency and structure

There has also been some change in thinking about these issues, for example within the social sciences. Rather than seeing human agency, on the one hand, and the constraints of social and natural structures, on the other, in a binary opposition, as if the two were separate and distinct, there has been a move towards focusing upon the interrelationship between the two. Social and 'natural' structures are the outcome of human activities, as well as influencing the ways in which people act, and, in particular, constraining their actions. Structures such as the transformation of technologies can be liberating as well as constraining and it is apparent that the relationship between the actions of human agents and the structures which organize and frame their lives is not a simple one, nor one where structures are only constraining and limiting. This tension between the extent to which human beings shape their own lives and experience and the extent to which they are constrained is not a new debate. It has a long history within philosophy and the social sciences. This debate frequently leads to the classification of social thinkers as favouring one side or the other of the agency/structure dualism. However, more recently the argument has focused upon the tension and balances between the two elements and the need to address both as inextricably involved in any study of human societies. Structures emerge and are classified through the activities of human beings. Even 'natural' structures are closely interconnected with human activity, either as a result of the impact of human activity upon 'nature' or through the categorization of particular phenomena. In the case of disability this is illustrated by the ways in which people with disabilities have been disadvantaged by the organization of the societies in which they live, by a 'disabling environment' rather than by disabled bodies. Another aspect of this which has been indicated in this chapter is the ways in which people are categorized and represented, for example in the language which is used to describe and identify them.

The relationship between agency and structure is transformed at particular historical moments and the balance between structural changes and their transformation through human agency shifts. Debates about citizenship in recent years offer particularly useful examples of the impact of collective agency and of the emergence of new forms of political organization, some of which are specific to their historical context.

Summary

- The interrelationship between agency and structure is an important element in framing debates within the social sciences.
- Debates about citizenship raise the issue of the tension and relationship between agency and structure as part of the explanations offered by the social sciences.
- Changes in the experience and understanding of citizenship illustrate the impact of collective action upon social structures.
- Although the structures of race, gender and disability constrain individuals and prevent their full participation in citizenship, these structures can be affected and transformed by the collective activity of people involved.

Thinking again about evaluation

The discussion up to this point has illustrated some of the ways in which citizenship raises important issues within the social sciences and in contemporary life. The big issue of who is included and who is excluded in social life is hotly debated in terms of the causes of exclusion and definitions of what constitutes citizenship, as well as what action might be taken in order to redress inequalities. We have looked at some of the different dimensions of citizenship and at some of the areas of exclusion. This has required a focus on some of the structures which constrain particular groups of people from full participation as well as some of the areas in which change has taken place, for example as a result of collective action. Since the area is clearly one of contestation how can we use this material to present some evaluation? What does the more detailed discussion of other approaches and additional evidence contribute to the assessment of the discussion of citizenship in the section above on 'Who is a citizen?' If we reconsider Marshall's definition of citizenship and his argument about equality, might the discussion in the section 'The challenge of other arguments' offer any new analysis?

ACTIVITY

Take each of the questions posed in 'Weighing up the argument' and reconsider the claims that citizenship is based on equality and that all citizens should be treated equally. Consider these questions in the light of the different issues in 'The challenge of other arguments'.

1   What is the evidence which supports this claim being made?
2   Does the claim cover all the situations and people involved or are there any people left out?
3   Do the conclusions follow from the initial premises and does it make sense?

COMMENT

1   Parekh's examples of the experience of people from the diverse ethnic groups which make up European societies like the UK, suggest specific instances where equal treatment would lead to inequality and exclusion. Similarly, evidence of racial violence makes it apparent that difference has to be addressed in all its manifestations in order to produce an inclusive citizenship. Other aspects of difference such as gender and generation also challenge the argument that full citizenship has to be based on equal treatment. For example women's interrupted patterns of paid work lead to increased poverty in old age in a welfare system that is based on eligibility for a pension derived from continuous contributions made through the uninterrupted life of paid employment.

2   All the groups of people, many of whom belong in several of the different categories covered in 'The challenge of other arguments', may be outside the norm of citizenship that the liberal approach based on equality assumes. Even Marshall's view which encompasses class differences cannot accommodate the diversity of the experience of ethnic minorities, women, disabled people and people at different points in the life course, often the elderly and retired. In the case of people with disabilities it is often the model of disability which leads to their exclusion from full citizenship. For example the medical model of disability positions disabled people as victims and as dependents. The excesses of the social model may underplay physical problems and again overlook or marginalize the contributions and participation of people who have some form of disability.

3   In one sense equal treatment follows logically from the assumption that everyone is equal to start with. However, even Marshall's account, does not start with an equal playing field. As Marshall points out, capitalist industrialized societies are characterized by inequalities, which full citizenship has to redress. Once there is the recognition of difference there has to be different treatment, that is different policies in order to achieve fuller, more active participation in civil and political life.

Conclusion

This chapter has addressed the issue of citizenship as an example of a big issue in contemporary societies, which revolves around questions of inclusion and exclusion; that is who participates and who is excluded or marginalized from civil, political and social life. Debates about citizenship have recently focused on discussion about equality and the advisability or not of policies that advocate equal treatment. The idea of equal treatment has been countered by the notion of difference and the need to accommodate differences such as those of ethnicity, gender, generation and disability. The idea of difference has been deployed to indicate the ways in which equal treatment fails to respond to the specific needs of particular groups. For example one of the ways in which women have been excluded from full participation as citizens has been their absence from paid work or their interrupted working lives. This has meant that women have not been able to make the necessary contributions, for example to receive a pension at the end of their working lives. Similarly women may not have been entitled to unemployment pay in the past because of the greater likelihood that they were working part time, and thus did not have the necessary record of insurance. An approach that focuses upon difference as well as seeking greater equality in outcomes, can address some of these issues, notably by taking on board the specific needs of hitherto marginalized groups. An understanding of difference also leads to a more thorough examination of what is considered to be the 'normal citizen'. Is this category an able-bodied, white man who is able to engage in full-time paid work throughout his adult life course? As has been suggested, frequently other aspects of citizenship have been dependent on the assumptions of who is the 'normal citizen'.

In changing times, there are increased movement and migration across state boundaries, as well as social, cultural, political and economic changes in families, work and everyday life. Some of the transformations of contemporary life have highlighted the importance of rethinking what it means to be a citizen, and in particular to draw attention to those who may still be denied full citizenship rights. This analysis has employed some of the structures which interact with personal experience and illustrate the ways in which human agency is both shaped by and influences social, political, cultural and economic structures. Some of the changes that have taken place in our understanding of citizenship and in the experience of being a citizen, have resulted from collective action. This is an area which has been the focus of political action both within the mainstream of party politics and of what has been called identity politics. Identity politics arising out of the new social movements of the late 1960s led to demands by the women's movement, gay and lesbian rights movements, organizations promoting rights based on issues of race and ethnicity and the disability movement, for full citizenship rights.

The discussion in this chapter has also focused on some of the strategies adopted within the social sciences for the evaluation of different approaches and theoretical perspectives. Whilst in this chapter we have applied some of the criteria employed and questions posed to the example of citizenship and in particular to debates about equality and difference, these strategies have wider implications which relate to all of the big issues addressed in this book, especially in the interconnections between structure and agency and the role of collective action in effecting political changes. Citizenship offers a good example of both contemporary debates about social change and the transformation of societies in the twenty-first century and about the role of collective action in effecting change.

Chapter 4

Buying and selling

Introduction

> The great afternoon rush-hour had arrived, when the overheated machine led the dance of customers, extracting money from their very flesh. In the silk department especially there was a sense of madness . . . In the still air, where the stifling central heating brought out the smell of the materials, the hubbub was increasing, made up of all sorts of noises – the continuous trampling of feet, the same phrase repeated a hundred times at the counters, gold clinking on the brass cash-desks, besieged by a mass of purses, the baskets on wheels with their loads of parcels falling endlessly into the gaping cellars.
>
> (Zola 1995: 108–9)

What is this about? It is a description of a shopping experience which has resonance with many in the contemporary western world. The reference to the silk department might be a giveaway of earlier times, as might the mention of gold and purses. Nowadays it would be more likely to be ready-made designer label clothes and the swiping of credit cards! However, Emile Zola's novel *The Ladies' Paradise* captures a historical moment and, with the arrival of the department store, the modernization of commercial activities. The historical moment is the middle of the nineteenth century when the Bon Marche department store opened in Paris. There were parallel developments in the United States and in England. Although the advent of such large-scale shops meant the demise of traditional family stores, as recorded in the novel, Zola's novel is a celebration of the activity of modernity and in a sense a 'hymn to modern business, a celebration of the entrepreneurial spirit' (Nelson 1995: xi). The department store is the signifier of the promise of capitalism as experienced in the life of the city and for the middle classes. The store is a model for the capitalist economic system, based on the exchange of goods for profit. It is characterized by the principles of speed of turnover, circulation, commodity exchange and the rapid renewal of capital in the form of commodities.

The store and its surrounding arcades presented spaces for the display and sale of commodities, dreams and desires. These commodities which had initially promised to fulfil desires, now created them. This is an important shift in the process of consumption, and the links between production and consumption, which this chapter explores. The department store was first created to display products, but also to provide a space in which the fashionable public could display themselves. In a sense the commercial principle became displaced by the principle of seduction. This seduction of the consumer, notably of women as consumers, is the subject of Zola's novel. The novel covers a whole range of seduction techniques ranging from advertising, which was not a common practice in the nineteenth century, to free entry to the store, allowing customers to look without buying and to be seen, thus creating the idea and practice of shopping as a leisure activity. Prices were fixed, thus eliminating the interaction of bartering. The process of purchase became quick and impersonal. The physical layout of the store was deliberately organized to ensure that shoppers passed through the different departments, having to travel the length and breadth of the store to find what they had come to buy. The most significant mechanism of seduction described by Zola, is the seduction of the spectacle with the excesses of visual pleasure, using light, space, colour (sometimes overwhelmingly white) and glass to present luxurious exotic fabrics both within the store and in its window displays. Women are the main protagonists in the novel, although the management and ownership of the store are in men's hands. Mouret, the owner of Zola's Ladies Paradise is described by the novelist as so successful in his creation of desire for the commodities for sale in his store, because of his understanding of seduction, as well as of the capitalist system. On the first point 'Mouret's sole passion was the conquest of Woman. He wanted her to be queen in his shop: he had built his temple for her in order to hord her at his mercy. His tactics were to intoxicate her with amorous attentions, to trade on her desires' (1995: 234). There is some degree of poetic licence, given that this is a fictional account, but it does convey the necessary strength of the creation of desire for goods so that they become important in satisfying desires rather than only serving a particular use function, that is of having use value. On the second point, Mouret's success resulted from his understanding of the capitalist principle of economic exchange and circulation and his grasp of the need to utilize another new, transport system. Improved transport through roads in the city and the development of the railway network in the nineteenth century greatly facilitated travel and the rapid circulation of goods both within the city of Paris and with the rest of the world. Thus development of a new and successful economic system is linked to technological advances. New modes of transport, the development of commodity culture and the importance of exchange value (rather than simply use value, that is what you can do with the products you buy) all created new ways of seeing the world and new forms of interaction. It is the novel's emphasis on the links between individuals and the culture in which they live, especially its focus on desire as motivating the system of exchange, that gives it such contemporary resonance.

This brief discussion of a fictional account, but one that has been very important in exploring both the historical and more recent manifestations of consumption and shopping, has introduced a whole range of concepts that require further explanation.

The Ladies' Paradise is set against the background of the development of an economic system, namely that of capitalism, which provides the framework, albeit in a variety of guises, for much of economic life around the globe, especially following the breakup of the former USSR and the former Eastern Europe. Capitalism involves a system of wage labour, whereby people provide their labour to an employer in return for payment, wages. It also features commodity production for sale and exchange, that is, people make things to sell, not only for their own use; most significantly, production and exchange are carried out for profit. The motivating force behind capitalist production is the creation of profit. Capital is created through the purchase of commodities. These are raw materials, machinery and labour. The combination of these elements creates a new commodity which is then sold – that is exchange value – for a price higher than it cost to produce, thus making a profit. Karl Marx argued that it was because labour had become a commodity and labour was exploited – workers are paid less than the value their work creates for the capitalist – that profit is produced which creates more capital for use by the owners of the means of production. The Marxist approach was very influential in the nineteenth and first half of the twentieth centuries but it has been much less explicitly acknowledged in recent times. It has been suggested that Marx's view of the class system is too simplistic and that the working class has become better off, not impoverished as Marx predicted. However, class plays a crucial part in the life chances of people in all modern societies, ranging from health, to education, and life expectancy to consumption and employment. Marxism stresses the role of production, its exploitation of workers – that is of labour – and the way in which production determines what is made and hence what is bought, that is consumed. Have times changed? People in the west, especially, now live in what has been termed the 'consumer society'. Advertising and marketing are so embedded in western cultures that it may be taken for granted that 'we are what we buy', and consumption shapes social relations and social divisions. People are marked out as different from each other according to the goods they purchase (or cannot purchase, because they lack the resources to do so), rather than societies being differentiated by the ways in which production is organized. Before we look at these arguments in more detail I want to map out some of the ideas which came before these claims that there has been a massive shift towards the 'consumer society'.

Processes of production and consumption

Class

The concept of class provides a most useful means of both describing and explaining inequalities, social divisions and change. Without going as far as Karl Marx and claiming that all history is the history of class struggle (see below), the notion of class has been deployed by large numbers of social scientists through the nineteenth and twentieth centuries to incorporate a number of the ways in which groups of people have both very different and unequal experiences, and different perceptions about their position in the wider society. Class involves the division of people into different groups according to their wealth, or lack of it, occupations and life chances. Factors such as sources of income, family background, education, place of residence, political affiliations and cultural tastes have all been invoked as part of the explanatory framework. However, there are key components of class, which make it such a useful tool for understanding social change. Classes are grounded in some shared material position, which is linked to the work people do and how they are rewarded for their labour. Class involves an emphasis on a shared, common position, which similarity of experience gives rise to some commonality of perception and outlook. Class is about shared experience deriving from common conditions. Some of this commonality of interests can give rise to political action and the impetus for political organization, for example in political parties or collective groups like trades unions or other such groups committed to action and social change. The processes of production have been given high priority in definitions of class.

As Marx wrote in the *Communist Manifesto*, in 1848, of the bourgeoisie, that is the capitalist class, whose class position derived from their ownership of the means of production: 'The bourgeoisie, during its scarce one hundred years has created more massive and colossal productive forces than have all preceding generations together' (in Feuer 1959: 12). Times have changed and Marx could not have predicted the scale of contemporary globalization, or its complexity. Changing times have led to different approaches to class and even challenges to the usefulness of the concept.

At points in the twentieth century it was claimed that class no longer mattered and other social divisions had superseded class. Such views were based on several different assumptions and different sources of evidence. For example it was suggested that the economic basis of class differences had been eroded. The decline of heavy manufacturing industry and the increase in service sector work had led to a democratization of the workforce, where it was no longer possible to differentiate clearly between blue and white collar workers. The conditions of work no longer gave rise to easily distinguishable attitudes, experience and performance. It was also claimed that political action has increasingly become organized around other areas of difference, such as gender, ethnicity, sexuality, disability and issues linked to the environment and the perception of risk, rather than traditional class interests. The other dimension of this debate, which we will look at in more detail in 'Consumer societies' below, is the argument that consumption has assumed greater importance in shaping attitudes and perceptions. This is linked to the claim that production and consumption are interrelated, rather than separate and distinct, and that production should not be seen as the most important factor in shaping social divisions and inequalities.

Inequality

There has been some resurgence of interest of the concept of class especially in explaining large-scale patterns of inequality, for example across the globe, where differences in quality of life are enormous between the rich countries of the west and parts of the developing world. Economic inequalities between countries have not only widened between the different parts of the world. They have increased within Europe for example, and within European countries, with the spread of modern capitalism, especially since the breakup of the former USSR. According to the UN Development Programme there has been 'The fastest rise in inequality ever. Russia now has the greatest inequality – the income share of the richest 20 per cent is 11 times that of the poorest 20 per cent' (Callinicos 2000: 2). There is also considerable inequality among UK citizens. Evidence of relative earnings is one measure of inequality. Which are the highest and lowest paid occupations in Britain? Which jobs receive the lowest wages?

Table 4.1 shows that treasurers and company financial managers earning an average of £1,059 a week, topped the earnings league in April 2000. Bottom of the league were kitchen porters and bar staff with an average of £184 a week, which is less than a fifth of the earnings of the top groups.

Table 4.1 Earnings by occupation, Great Britain, April 2000

	Average gross weekly pay (£)
Highest paid	
Treasurers and company financial managers	1,059
Medical practitioners	964
Organization and methods and work study managers	813
Management consultants, business analysts	812
Underwriters, claims assessors, brokers, investment analysis	775
Police officers (inspector or above)	766
Computer systems and data processing managers	757
Solicitors	748
Marketing and sales managers	719
Advertising and public relations managers	690
Lowest paid	
Educational assistants	212
Other childcare and related occupations	205
Counterhands, catering assistants	196
Launderers, dry cleaners, pressers	196
Hairdressers, barbers	190
Waiters, waitresses	189
Petrol pump, forecourt attendants	189
Retail cash desk and check-out operators	185
Bar staff	184
Kitchen porters, hands	184

Source: New Earnings Survey, Office for National Statistics.

£ per week

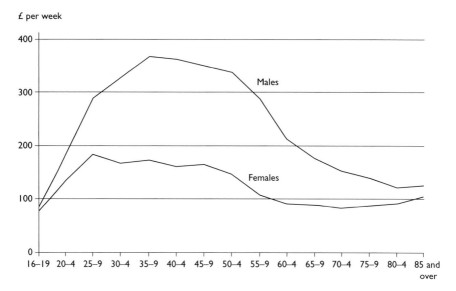

Figure 4.1 Median individual gross income, by gender and age, Great Britain, 1999–2000

Source: Family Resources Survey, Department for Work and Pensions.

There are also differences between women's and men's earnings. Figure 4.1 gives the median, gross (that is before tax and other deductions such as National Insurance) earnings. The median is the midpoint of the distribution or spread, a halfway point with 50 per cent above this line and 50 per cent below. What do you notice about the differences in the earnings of women and men? Do the differences vary across different age groups?

Figure 4.1 shows that men earned more than women in all age groups in the year from 1999 to 2000, although age is an important factor. The closest group is the 16 to 19-year-olds with young women earning £76 a week and young men £83. Other factors impinge upon earnings in retirement for the older age group and it is worth noting that there are more women than men in the over 80 categories.

Ownership of wealth is another indicator of inequality within a society. What does Figure 4.1 tell us about the distribution of wealth in Britain in the late 1990s? How even is the distribution of wealth? What might this tell us about inequality?

Wealth is less evenly distributed than income. It is difficult to assess the wealth of individuals, especially as the assets of the very rich can be most diffusely spread and not simple to measure. Table 4.2 represents a picture of a moment, rather than wealth ownership through the life course of individuals. However, it is estimated that 1 per cent of individuals owned between one-fifth and one-quarter of total wealth. Perhaps more alarmingly, at the other end of the scale 50 per cent of the population shared only 6 per cent of total wealth. Whilst not being definitive this

Table 4.2 Wealth ownership, UK (%)[a]

	1976	1981	1986	1991	1996	1997	1998	1999
Marketable wealth								
Percentage of wealth owned by:[b]								
Most wealthy 1%	21	18	18	17	20	22	23	23
Most wealthy 5%	38	36	36	35	40	43	43	43
Most wealthy 10%	50	50	50	47	52	54	55	54
Most wealthy 25%	71	73	73	71	74	75	75	74
Most wealthy 50%	92	92	90	92	93	93	94	94
Total marketable wealth (£ bn)	280	565	955	1,711	2,092	2,248	2,594	2,752
Marketable wealth less value of dwellings								
Percentage of wealth owned by:[b]								
Most wealthy 1%	29	26	25	29	26	30	32	34
Most wealthy 5%	47	45	46	51	49	54	58	58
Most wealthy 10%	57	56	58	64	63	66	70	71
Most wealthy 25%	73	74	75	80	81	83	85	86
Most wealthy 50%	88	87	89	93	94	95	96	97

Source: Inland Revenue.

Notes
a Estimates for individual years should be treated with caution as they are affected by sampling error and the particular pattern of deaths in that year.
b Adults aged 18 and over.

does paint a picture of an inegalitarian society, with considerable inequity in the distribution of wealth and resources. One of the most common ways of identifying inequality and more specifically poverty in any society is to consider the situation of children. Child poverty is an important indicator of inequality. For Britain the evidence suggests that there has been an increase in child poverty over the past three decades. This is measured by household income, for example if the household in which children are living has an income below the average wage. In Britain in 1979, 9 per cent of children lived in households with an income below the average, by 1996 this had increased to 35 per cent (Department of Social Security 1998).

Marx and class

The history of all hitherto existing society is the history of class struggles. Free man and slave, patrician and plebeian, lord and serf, guild master and journeyman, in a word, oppressor and oppressed, stood in constant opposition to one another, carried on an uninterrupted, now hidden, now open fight, a fight that each time ended in either a revolutionary re-constitution of society at large or in the common ruin of the contending classes . . .

Our epoch, the epoch of the bourgeoisie, possesses, however this distinctive feature: it has simplified class antagonisms. Society as a whole is more and more splitting into two great hostile camps, into two great classes directly facing each other; bourgeoisie and proletariat . . .

The bourgeoisie cannot exist without constantly revolutionizing the means of production, and thereby the relations of production, and with them the whole relations of society . . .

The need of a constantly expanding market for its products chases the bourgeoisie over the whole surface of the globe . . . by the rapid movement of all instruments of production, by the immensely facilitated means of communication, draws all . . . nations into civilization.

(Marx and Engels in Feuer 1959: 7–11)

'The essential condition for the existence of the bourgeois class . . . is the formation and augmentation of capital; the condition for capital is wage labour' (ibid.: 19). These quotations from the *Communist Manifesto* by Kark Marx (1818–83) and Friedrich Engels (1820–95) makes a strong statement about the primacy of social class. Indeed, for Marx, class was the motivating force behind social change and the primary social division. Class position derived from people's relationship to the means of production, as owners or as those reduced to selling their labour. Thus production is more important than consumption and the particular form of production in any society determines social relations. In a capitalist society this means that ownership of capital and commodity production creates two main classes: the bourgeoisie, who own the means of production; and the proletariat, who sell their labour for a wage. Whilst there may be more complex social divisions which may cross class boundaries, class and the socio-economic positions it shapes, remains a key factor in the formation of experience and social relations. Marx's focus was on inequality. He emphasized the material aspects of inequality. This inequality, he argued, would become more polarized as capitalism developed. The proletariat, he predicted, would become ever more impoverished. Class consciousness was also very important to Marx's argument, which concentrated on the working class or proletariat becoming sufficiently aware of its collective class predicament as a class 'for itself', ultimately to take action to overthrow the dominance of the bourgeoisie and the capitalist system.

Weber and class

We may speak of a 'class' when (1) a number of people have in common a specific causal component of their life chances, in so far as (2) this component is represented exclusively by accompanying interests in the possession of goods and opportunities for income, and (3) is represented under the conditions of the commodity or labour markets.

(Weber in Gerth and Mills 1948: 181)

Thus Max Weber (1864–1920) sees class situation as reflecting life chances which are themselves determined by the market and by people's position in relation to the market. The sort of factors that would shape life chances would be ownership of property, skills and education. Whereas Marx identified two main classes, set in conflict against each other, Weber paints a broader picture, listing these groups as social classes:

- The working class
- The petty bourgeoisie, for example small shopkeepers
- Technicians, specialists and lower management
- The classes privileged through property and education, that is those who occupy the top positions and are at the top of the class hierarchy.

Weber lays no claim to the importance or existence of class consciousness. He presents an argument which distinguishes between class, status and party, but acknowledges that the three elements interrelate and overlap. Economic class and social class are not necessarily linked. It is possible to have status, for example in relation to occupation, without the job carrying economic ranking. In many ways Weber's account of social classes is not so very different from Marx's, especially in terms of describing classes in a capitalist society. He identifies similar areas of difference between socio-economic groups. However, whereas Marx's two classes are defined *in relation* to each other – the bourgeoisie cannot exist without the proletariat and vice versa – Weber's classes exist as a hierarchy.

Weber both concentrates on market position, including the paid work which people do and adds other dimensions to this explanation of social divisions and stratification. One of these is status which may or may not align with occupational hierarchies. Status brings in a more complex picture of social divisions, although it may still be more descriptive than explanatory in its contribution to the debate.

Summary: differences between Marx and Weber

- For Marx class is grounded in the exploitation and domination which are an essential part of the relations of *production*, whereas for Weber class reflects life chances in the market.
- Marx's definition of class is based on the relationship of different groups of people to the means of production and to each other. Thus it is a relational explanation, whereas Weber's account is based on a description of hierarchies that are shaped by life chances and market relations.
- Marx gives priority to class as the most influential aspect of historical development. For Marx class conflict motivates historical change, whereas for Weber it is not the prime motivator of change.
- For Marx class action is inevitable, whereas for Weber class is only one

aspect of society which may present a possible motivation for action and change but the link is neither inevitable nor the only factor to consider.

- Although Weber incorporates status into his analysis of social divisions, production still plays a key role in the creation of class in many accounts. There is also a separation of production and consumption and a greater emphasis on production, but things have changed.

Consumer society?

ACTIVITY

Read this short extract from a newspaper article about the fashion chain Zara. The chain has been very successful. The company has opened stores in forty-four countries, including Russia, in 2002. Zara is worn by the cognoscenti, what Caroline Roux, in her article, along with many fashion journalists, calls the 'fashionista'. The Zara shops specialize in supplying designer clothes at high street prices. The clothes are worn by media celebrities and fashion journalists as well as thousands of fashion and budget conscious shoppers. They bring together high fashion (Bond Street) with popular high street (Oxford Street). The company's Spanish owner occupies the number 25 spot on the Forbes' billionaire list, with a $9.1bn fortune. He is the richest man in Spain, but keeps a very low profile. The company is enormously successful in spite of spending very little on advertising, with a marketing budget only 4 per cent of overall expenditure (Roux 2002: 6).

> What it has done is plug a gap in the market with a desirable product: high fashion for middle-class urban women . . .
> Zara's largest European store – a 3,000 sq. m. temple to consumption opened in Oxford Street and Bond Street, its locations rather conveniently summing up Zara's knack for offering high-style clothes at high-street prices . . . The building was completely concealed beneath hoardings with no indication of who was about to launch themselves into the Oxford Street mêlée. Rumours abounded. By the time the store was ready, the Zara faithful had spread the word.
> Within minutes of the doors opening, the tills were ringing and shoppers leaving laden with easily identifiable navy paper bags . . .
> The speed at which Zara translates catwalk styles into high-street products is the key to its success. It can do this because it controls manufacturing more closely than any of its competitors . . . by producing 50 per cent of its product in-house.
> If a style doesn't sell well within a week, it is withdrawn.
> (Roux 2002: 6)

What parallels are there with the extract from *The Ladies' Paradise* at the start of this chapter? How does the Zara phenomenon illustrate the claim that consumption shapes experience and social relations? What might be missing in this account?

COMMENT

In many ways this account, written in 2002, has resonance with Zola's fictional narrative written one and a half centuries earlier. The emphasis is still on profit, whether it is tills ringing or gold clinking. The profit machine is in motion. Some of the marketing strategies are the same and the new Zara store is described exotically as a 'temple to consumption' very like the Ladies' Paradise department store. The contemporary article mirrors the excitement surrounding the promotion of these products in much the same way that Zola conjures up the advent of department stores in the nineteenth century.

Interestingly, in the twenty-first century this relatively new venture, whilst generating massive profits, does not devote much resource to advertising per se. However, there are other strategies, all linked to promotion. The publicity accorded media stars and fashion icons, all of whom admit publicly to wearing Zara is a less direct strategy. It is nonetheless very much part of the product promotion strategy. Similarly, the shrouded building in Oxford Street lends very public mystique and fuel for the rumours and mystery which contribute to the excitement associated with the product. Whilst the goods may be at 'high street prices', not everyone is included in this fashion bonanza. It is exclusive culturally and to some extent economically. What is missing is exclusion and inequality. The gap in the market it purports to fill, is to cater for 'middle-class urban women'. This is an already somewhat privileged group of consumers. The cost of Zara products is low compared with designer goods, not with the clothes from charity shops or the really cheap items that are possibly more within the spending power of the poorest groups of women. Low cost, however, allows for high turnover for the company and for its fashion-conscious consumers, whose wardrobes can be renewed frequently to fit in with the demands of contemporary culture.

The company has developed a series of very effective strategies which respond to contemporary patterns of consumption. Speed is of the essence in the fast-changing climate of fashion as the Zara company acknowledges by translating catwalk styles into accessible high street products more quickly than its competitors. The company also retains its competitive edge by controlling its production at its own factories rather than tendering to other suppliers.

The production and consumption processes are clearly closely interconnected. Production is geared to the needs and demands of consumers within the market for fashionable clothes at reasonable prices. This company has found its moment and has carved out a more profitable, substantial niche in the market. Its fashions are represented through the association with attractive media celebrities as well as with the culture of cool in everyday life. Buying into this culture and the identities it constructs becomes possible for consumers, who are able to purchase affordable fashion, which nonetheless connotes a style which might be associated with afflu-ence. This notion of the interrelationships between different points in the processes of production and consumption draws upon an idea introduced by Richard Johnson and developed by Paul du Gay and Stuart Hall in the 'circuit of culture' (1997). This 'circuit' illustrates five moments in the process of production of cultural texts and artefacts, like fashion. Figure 4.2 shows how the circuit operates and how the processes interrelate.

This model is useful for indicating stages or moments in the process of the making and exchange of products. The circuit also gives primacy to the cultural production of meanings about products. Culture is implicated in the whole process. Representation involves the ways in which meanings are presented, through images, language and practices. This is a moment in the circuit that has particular resonance with the world of fashion. Fashion is intrinsically and necessarily the product of representational systems, which convey and create meanings about what is in and what is out, and which are the 'must haves' of the moment. Representations include the images in magazines, on television, through popular culture, especially images of celebrities, as well as the fashion channel, films and the Internet. Identities are the subject positions into which people who buy the product are recruited. Fashion creates its desirable and desiring subjects through representational systems. The fashion industry depends on consumers buying into the identities which it promotes by buying its products. Production involves the raw materials, labour, time, machines and technologies that combine in the creation of artefacts and services. In the fashion industry this involves new technologies in the creation of new styles, fabrics and designs. Fashion depends heavily on change and on the idea of the 'new'. New approaches are implicated at all levels, in the

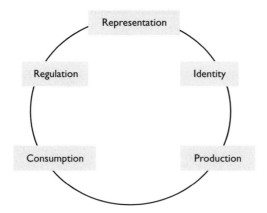

Figure 4.2 The circuit of culture
Source: du Gay *et al.* 1997: 3.

representations deployed, the identities constructed, and in the processes and technologies of production. Consumption refers to the exchange and services and the point at which they are purchased and consumed. This is the point at which the consumers are recruited into the identities by buying the product and we find out if the new technologies and the strategies used to promote the product have worked. Regulation involves the ways in which the public and private spheres of life are linked in the governance and control of production and consumption. This operates in myriad ways. Some involve the regulation of employment in the industry. Fashion is an industry with a long history of out-working, home-working and the exploitation of low paid workers both within countries like the UK and in different parts of the world, where wages are low. There is also regulation of the fabrics used, including fur and animal products, and of the ways in which these can be promoted. In some of the glossy, more up-market magazines, there has been considerable controversy about the representation of models in states of undress, smoking cigarettes and at one time displaying what was called 'heroin chic' through emaciated bodies and darkened eyes. The representation of fashion is implicated in a range of moral discourses about what is acceptable and what is not, especially in the context of its appeal for an ever-younger market. Regulation of styles, practices and processes are all involved in deciding what it is acceptable to wear, when and by whom.

What is most important for our purposes here is the interrelationship between production and consumption. This is partly what challenges more traditional views of the primacy of production and the idea that production shaped consumption. How far have we moved the other way, even to the extent of claiming that consumption is dominant? Steve Spittle suggests that: 'We seem to have less interest in wider social issues and more interest in the consumption-based lifestyles offered to us by television and commercial markets' (2002: 58). He is writing about television programming and the preference of viewers for consumption-based 'make-over' shows and consumer entertainment over news and documentary viewing. However, the point remains that consumption rules. Do you agree with this claim?

There is empirical evidence of increased consumer spending in affluent western countries. In the west, household expenditure has soared in recent years and there is massive spending on a wide range of consumer goods. This would certainly support the argument that there has been a massive expansion in consumer goods and in their purchase. Much of this spending is made using credit cards.

Look at Figure 4.3 which gives details of the types of purchase that are made by credit and debit cards. In which areas is consumer spending highest using plastic? Which sort of cards do people use for different purchases?

These figures show that food and drink purchases for supermarkets, off-licences and general stores rank highest in debit card spending, accounting for £24 billion in 2000. This is twice the debit card spending in any other category and approximately one-third of all debit card spending. One of the reasons people may use debit cards in supermarkets is that they are able to get cash back on a debit card

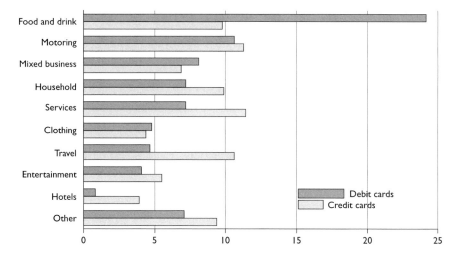

Figure 4.3 Credit[a] and debit[b] card spending by type of purchase, UK, 2000 (£ bn)

Source: Credit Card Research Group.

Notes
a Mastercard and Visa cards only.
b Visa and Switch cards only.

but not on a credit card, and this is an ever more common practice. Travel and holiday spending is more likely to involve a credit card payment. This kind of evidence does highlight some of the patterns of consumer spending and the practices that are implicated in the 'consumer society'.

Does an expansion in consumption necessarily mean that we live in a consumer society, or that consumption largely takes place for its own sake, or for lifestyle reasons rather than for the immediate use of the goods purchased? Much of UK consumption is on housing and cars. Entertainment forms a significant proportion of consumer spending with IT and media equipment high on the list (*Social Trends* 2002: 209). Consumers are certainly very active in that there is a great deal of consuming going on! Goods and services are being purchased. However, this does not necessarily mean that consumers are exercising a great deal of choice and autonomy. It is possible for consumption to be shaped by forces outside the consumer's control. How far do consumers resist the pressure from producers who may attempt to foist upon them products that are not wanted? Clearly some products fail, however much effort is put into their promotion. Consumers are not passive dupes and exercise considerable control through their own actions, in buying or rejecting goods and services. However, if we look at the wider arena, there is also resistance to globalization through anti-globalization movements and green politics and campaigns against the massive environmental destruction which has arisen from the huge increase in consumption worldwide. Some of the challenges, especially in the context of globalization, are explored in Chapter 6.

Different approaches to the consumer society

Steve Spittle (2002) argues that market-based consumption dominates affluent western countries like the UK. Everywhere we look there is information about consumer products, in all media, in the street and on the Internet. Kalle Lasn suggests

> Advertising and marketing are so deeply embedded in our culture now that it's hard to imagine a time when product placement and network logo and 'burns' and 'bugs' weren't everywhere you looked, when our lifestyles and culture weren't predicated on consumption. But that pre-marketing era was not so long ago: only two generations.
>
> (Lasn 2000: 421–2)

This move to the consumer society is seen here as a relatively recent phenomenon, but it has become one that is taken for granted in the west. It has become part of 'who we are' and what we expect. Much television programming focuses largely on the promotion of products and services, not only through the frequent advertising on the commercial channels, but also through some of the most popular programmes. Make-over programmes, whether of our houses, our gardens, our bodies or our psyches and relationships, all advocate the need to be constantly changing and re-forming. We are exhorted to review ourselves and our lives; who we are as indicated by what we own, what we do and how we do it. The constant re-production of ourselves, our homes and our gardens requires knowledge, products and services and especially the knowledge of which products to employ in this ongoing quest.

This kind of approach reflects some of the postmodernist views of the consumer society. Such approaches stress the importance of representational systems. The commodity, that is the goods produced for sale through the combination of raw materials, machinery, technologies and labour, have been replaced by the 'commodity sign'. This means that what the commodity stands for, what it represents and how it is represented have overtaken its use value. Things are not bought to be used only, but for what they represent. So, Zara fashions mean cool, streetwise chic, Coke means freedom and energy. You will be able to think of many other examples. The message is usually stated either explicitly or by association in the advertisements for the products. These associations are not only deployed to persuade us to buy the product, they become the product and this is what we are buying into. In this sense the system is based not on the desire for material goods as much as for the meanings associated with them and the different meanings between products. Consumer goods have thus become the source of meaning in society, rather than other identifications, such as the community within which we live, our families, religious groups or work-based affiliations. This argument was put forward by writers such as Jean Baudrillard: 'What is sociologically significant for us, and what marks our era under the sign of consumption, is precisely the generalised reorganisation of this primary level in a system of signs which appears to be . . . the specific mode of our era' (1988: 47). However, this may be an overstatement, especially of the symbolic aspects of consumption. Postmodernism lays a heavy emphasis on the role of the symbolic and on how commodities and artefacts are represented through signs. We are certainly bombarded with signs in our everyday lives, but the influence of these signs and their dominance in constructing meaning in our lives and in social relations can be overstated. As we saw in Chapter 2, Pierre Bourdieu (1984) incorporates an analysis of taste and consumption into a class-based critique of social relations. He retains a material base and the notion of constraints and limitations, for example in the autonomy of consumers. As Bourdieu argues, although patterns of consumption form part of communications and classificatory systems, they are also deeply embedded in social structures especially of class. He argued that social class was the main determinant of consumption which clearly provides a material antidote to the excesses of some postmodernist accounts, which see the symbolic as the only relevant factor. Bourdieu argues that consumption is linked to social differentiation because 'taste classifies the classifier', that is what you buy classifies you. 'Social subjects, classified by their classifications, distinguish themselves by the distinctions they make, between the beautiful and the ugly, the distinguished and the vulgar, in which their position in the objective classification is expressed or betrayed' (ibid.: 6). For Bourdieu consumption is symbolic but it is also material. People's capacity to consume these goods refers to their material social position – including and most importantly their financial resources – and what he calls their *cultural capital*. Cultural capital includes what we have learned, for example from our parents and from our education, the sort of people we are.

Zygmunt Bauman also suggests a more constraining view of the free market consumer, picking and choosing an identity off the peg. He also points to the tendency in postmodernist approaches, not to distinguish between different aspects of consumption. It may not be that there has been such a radical shift from the dominance of production to that of consumption in shaping our lives and experiences, but that contemporary life is characterized by a new form of consumption. As Bauman argues,

> The distinctive mark of the consumer society and its consumerist culture is not, however, consumption as such; not even the elevated and fast rising volume of consumption. What sets the members of consumer society apart from their ancestors is the emancipation of consumption from its past instrumentality that used to draw its limits – the demise of 'norms' and the new plasticity of 'needs', setting consumption free from functional bonds and absolving it from the need to justify itself by reference to anything but its own pleasurability.
>
> (Bauman 2001: 12–13)

Bauman suggests that what has changed is the nature of consumption and what makes current patterns of consumption significant is the move towards an emphasis on the pleasure as well as the functional dimensions of consumption. As anthropologists like Danny Miller have pointed out, the consumption of goods has never been a purely functional activity and there is no sudden new departure into a realm of meaning which has hitherto been absent from human experience. Miller's argument is that objects and artefacts are not only imbued with meanings by those who use them but indicate their own material culture, that is a set of meanings which lies in the object, rather than merely being attributed to it by its users. Miller is critical of some of the postmodernist and sociological views of recent years.

> Sociologists, in particular, almost inevitably write about consumption as though contemporary society were a decline from some earlier state in which our main relationship to objects was constructed through some form of utility or need . . . it is extremely hard to find evidence for merely functional or utilitarian relations to material culture in any non-industrial society.
>
> (Miller 1995: 26)

Summary

- Previous approaches within the social sciences that stressed the separate stages of production and consumption have been challenged by more recent views which see the two as interrelated.
- The circuit of culture usefully maps out the ways different moments in cultural production and consumption interconnect.
- There has been a trend towards an emphasis on consumption rather than production as the key determinant of experience and of social relations.
- Postmodernism gives high priority to symbols and to representational systems seeing consumption as the main practice and area of experience shaping identities and social relations in the contemporary world.
- This view is challenged by more material approaches, one of which derives from the ideas of Bourdieu on the links between class and taste as expressed through patterns of consumption.
- The anthropological views of Miller take a material culture approach to consumption, and also challenge the notion that the creation of meaning through consumption is a new phenomenon.

Where is power?

In the above discussion there has been a tension between approaches to consumption which emphasize its importance as an expression of consumer choice and autonomy and the constraints which consumers experience. For example the Marxist view of class focuses on material inequalities and the greater power enjoyed by the capitalist class over the exploited working class because of the bourgeoisie's ownership of the means of production. In this case it is the capitalist class, the bourgeoisie, and the pursuit of profit that is required by the system, which determines what is produced, rather than any control that consumers themselves might exercise. In a theory which is based on the primacy of the production process ownership accords considerably more power to the group of owners than to those who sell their labour for a wage. Marx did argue that the power of the proletariat lay in its collective class position and its potential and realizable power to overthrow the capitalist system, but this power was difficult to exercise within that economic system. An understanding of power and its operations lies at the heart of any study of inequality and has some relevance for exploring the debates about the consumer society. Does power lie in the hands of the producers or in those of the consumers? What do we mean by power? Does power operate from the top down or are all human relations affected by some operations of power even in everyday exchanges? Do we associate it with people in power? Do we only think of power as involving a hierarchy?

ACTIVITY

Stop for a moment and think of two examples, either from your personal experience or from something that you have read about or seen or heard, where you think power is being exercised. This could be when you or someone were being compelled or maybe even persuaded to act in a way which was not your preference. Are there any examples in your own role as a consumer or in the experiences of other people? Perhaps you can think of an example of buying something which you did not really want to buy. Is power too strong a word in this case?

COMMENT

There may be some very obvious cases of pressure being exerted on the international scale, involving the military or, within a state, involving the police. You may have thought of examples of violence and the overt, explicit exercise of power. If you focused on the context of consumption, the exercise of power is likely to have been much less obvious. Perhaps a smooth-talking assistant persuaded you to buy something which was not really what you wanted. Maybe advertising was a force you could not resist, although most of us are unlikely to admit to that one. Advertising and fashion are extremely powerful in shaping our perception of what we want to buy. Conversely advertising may indicate how undesirable some items are. They may be associated with unacceptable, old-fashioned styles, which we are persuaded to avoid at all costs. Maybe you thought of some of the more sinister ways in which power is exercised over us as consumers. For example CCTV – closed-circuit television – acts as a surveillance device monitoring our progress through the shopping malls and precincts and inside shops. This is both a benefit and a constraint. CCTV is used to protect members of the public and store and property owners from criminal activity, but it also creates an environment in which everyone is constantly being watched.

Surveillance is a form of control, although it is difficult to identify the source of power. Who exactly is it who is exercising power here? You may feel that somebody is watching your every move but it is difficult to attribute agency to the camera. Another form of control in the context of consumption is the banks and credit-rating agencies. You may recall the process of verification, which many stores use in order to assess whether or not your cheque or credit card will be honoured. If you attempt to purchase items on credit the sales assistant will probably seek proof of your credit-worthiness from an agency. There are more material constraints, of course. You may have insufficient resources to make any purchases. You may not be able to buy into the consumer society because you have lost your job or are unable to work. Here the operation of power shifts beyond the local, perhaps to global economic forces. Your experience may be local and personal but the power that you lack has been exercised way outside your control, for example in the decision of an international company to close its plant in your home town so that you lose your job.

Some of the suggestions that I have made may seem surprising and you may have thought that persuasion is different from power. Power may be more associated with coercion or force. However, if we are persuaded to do something that it was not our intention to do, even if we were not entirely conscious of this happening it is likely that there has been some exercise of power, albeit indirectly. Many of the examples in the context of consumption illustrate this indirect operation of power, even at the level of the unconscious, for example in the case of advertisements.

How can we conceptualize power? What is involved? There has to be some notion of a relationship, whereby one side is not able to do what it wants and another side is able to exercise some control, whether these are conscious processes for both parties or not. Power may involve authority. Those with expertise may have authority which we lack because of lack of the relevant expert knowledge.

Power can be *direct*. Power can be exercised over others. Some people may have power on the basis of expertise, or superior resources or brute force. Others may be subjected to power because they lack these resources.

Power can be *indirect*. We may not notice what is going on. This is quite likely in the context of consumption. We may not purchase goods or services because of the unconscious meanings they carry (albeit arising from representations including advertisements) rather than from a conscious process, for example where we know that someone else is telling us what to do.

Common-sense notions of power, maybe as revealed in the above activity, are that it operates from the top down and that it may even involve coercion. The sociologist Max Weber argued that power is the probability that a person will be able to realize his – it was less likely to be her in Weber's analysis – objectives even against opposition from others (in Gerth and Mills 1948). This is not to say that Weber's analysis did not address gender, rather that he recognized women's lack of power in patriarchal societies. Weber is accredited with developing an analysis of patriarchy as one source of traditional authority. This concept has been very useful to subsequent feminist critiques, as a means of focusing upon some of the ways in which men exercise power over women.

Weber's initial definition of power is very broad, but he went on to be more specific. The main focus of Weber's theory of power was the power of the state over its people, rather than the exercise of power in everyday exchanges between people. He included domination, where people obey commands, and developed the idea of different strategies upon which the legitimacy of power depended, which he called 'ideal types' of legitimacy. He argued that power was the fundamental concept of social divisions, of which class, status and party were different dimensions. Class, as explained above, is the outcome of your position in the marketplace and your economic position, for example based on your occupation, thus covering economic power. Status involves the esteem in which you are held by others, thus covering social power, and party includes political affiliations, which meant political power. Power is thus the probability of people, as individuals or in groups, carrying out their will, even when opposed by others. In Weber's account, power largely operates in a top down way. It is organized through a series of rules and regulations, imposed by those in authority. It may not involve coercion, and is most often based on a chain of command, with authority being invested in those in the hierarchy who persuade others to comply with the rules through reasoned appeals to common sense and rationality. Weber's argument was developed to counter some of the oversimplifications of the nineteenth-century Marxist view, which could be read as overemphasizing economic power. He wanted to develop a more complex understanding of some of the ways in which power could be seen as operating in industrialized, capitalist societies, and to focus upon its operation in modern bureaucracies. Weber's approach permits some understanding of intention as well as conflict. His definition allows for someone, some agent or group of agents, to be carrying out their will. However, within institutions, whether public or private, Weber saw power as dependent upon an individual's position within the organization. It does seem to imply that those who are subordinate could resist the power which is exercised over them but the understanding of power involved here seems largely to be in the category of the more direct exercise of power, even if it can be challenged.

Other explanations of the operation of power provide more focus on the ways in which power might be more diffuse. It might be operating even in situations where there appears to be no conflict, nor even a chain of command, or specific source of authority. In the examples of persuasion that might be part of the experience of consumption, it is very difficult to state the source of power or even of authority. Are we in any way coerced or even explicitly persuaded to buy the goods, for example fashion items, that we say we want (whether or not we need them)?

Michel Foucault suggests that power is everywhere. As Foucault argues,

> Power is not something that is acquired seized or shared, something that one holds onto or allows to slip away, power is exercised from innumerable points, in the interplay of non-egalitarian and mobile relationship.
>
> Relations of power are not in a position of exteriority with respect to other relationships (economic processes, knowledge relationships, sexual relations) but are immanent in the latter . . .
>
> Power comes from below . . . in the machinery of production, in families, limited groups and institutions, are the basis for wide-ranging effects . . .
>
> Power relations are both intentional and nonsubjective . . . But this does not mean it results from choice or decision of an individual subject . . .
>
> Where there is power there is resistance . . . one is always 'inside' power, there is no 'escaping' it, there is no absolute outside where it is concerned.
>
> (Foucault 1981: 94–5)

Foucault's writing is quite difficult to follow and his argument is quite radical. He sees power as operating in all situations. We are all involved. He also claims that there is no 'exteriority' to it. That means that there is no source of power outside the way it is exercised. For example the Marxist argument claims that the source of power lies in economic conditions. Access to ownership of the means of production gives power to one class. It is possible to locate the source of power in these economic relations.

For Foucault, power operates at multiple points and it works through *discourse*. His use of the term is different from that in the common currency of everyday exchanges. He defines a discourse as involving all the practices, ideas and ways of thinking about something through which meanings are produced. A discourse presents a way of constructing meanings which organizes and influences what we do and how we see ourselves. A discourse is a set of knowledges and practices that create their own truth. A discourse is 'true' if it is taken to be true, not by virtue of being proved to be true or false in relation to something outside itself. Foucault cites the particular example of sexuality and sexual identities in his *History of Sexuality* (1981). What is the 'truth' about sexuality? In the case of sexual identities, meanings about sexuality do not derive from biology or from the mind, or the bodies we inhabit, but from the ways in which we describe, talk about and practise those feelings and activities which are categorized as sexual. For example heterosexuality or homosexuality are not the result of having either a particular sort of body, or a particular sort of mind. They result from the way in which the society – through knowledge, such as that produced by medical sources, the state through legislation, welfare and education systems – organizes and classifies what people do and what they feel and think. It is the process of categorization which creates the discourse. For example areas of expertise and authority, rather than depending on traditional hierarchies as in Weber's account, in Foucault's, present their own sets of meanings and truths.

Foucault extended his historical analysis of power to explore some of the ways in which discourses operate through subjects, that is how people are positioned by discourses *and* how they position themselves. A discourse not only makes it possible to think some things, it closes down other possibilities, so that we do not even consider some actions and thoughts.

Foucault moved on from an emphasis on discourse as producing particular kinds of subjects to argue that subjects also produce themselves, through particular practices. Foucault's examples often relate to the history of sexuality and the ways in which different practices and identities have been possible, 'put into discourse', at different times. For example he looked at the historical construction of sexual identities from fifth-century Athens to show men in ancient Greece engaged in different relationships with women and with other men, and the customs that permitted some practices and outlawed others. He claimed that what he called 'technologies of the self' enabled individuals to do things 'by their own means or with the help of others . . . so as to transform themselves in order to attain a certain state of happiness, purity, wisdom, perfection or immortality' (Foucault 1988: 18).

What is important about this argument is the way in which it puts people into discourse and allows the idea that practices and representations do not just operate outside us, shaping what we do, but we are also involved in the processes. To apply this notion of 'techniques of the self' to more recent practices of consumption we could look at both the ways in which meanings are produced through certain discourses, for example within popular culture, and the practices through which people produce themselves. The practices include shopping and spectatorship, the contemporary practice of spending quite extended periods of time 'at the shops', looking at the clothes and styles adopted by celebrities, engaging in discussion with friends and family and reading popular magazines. In the case of other areas of consumption the consumer seeks out different areas of expertise, perhaps more authoritative sources, from the Internet or even specialist literature, for example in the case of food and health products. Current representations of what it is possible to wear and what is appropriate in different situations and what valued, create what it is possible to think and possible to do. We can only think of particular items as desirable, designer labels, for example, because these meanings are created by contemporary discourses of fashion. They do not enter our heads. Domination works through self-control. We regulate ourselves, in many situations, rather than being coerced.

The notion of discourse might seem very well suited to our fashion and shopping example. In an ever-changing field like fashion it is more obvious that knowledge about what is acceptable and desirable is *produced*, rather than deriving from some external source. Clothing fashion is itself a discursive field. Consumers make purchases within this area of consumption according to the knowledge they have derived from magazines and popular culture and the influences of their peers. However, what constitutes a fashionable item may well be dictated by the producer. The Marxist emphasis on production would indeed have centred on the power exercised over consumers by the dominance of the producer and the capitalist class in shaping the practices of consumers. Foucault's more diffuse conception of power sees it operating at several different sites and not coming from one source. However, it may be more difficult to identify how meanings are produced through discourses when they are enmeshed and diffuse.

Summary

- An understanding of power and how it operates is crucial to the investigations of social scientists.
- Critiques of power take different positions about the sources of power and about how it operates.
- Weber's approach to the operation of power, based on hierarchies of authority in institutions, has been very influential.
- The Marxist approach has been challenged by approaches which place greater emphasis on *how* power operates than on its *sources*.
- Foucault's historical critique has stressed the diffuse nature of power and the mechanisms through which it operates.
- A major division lies between a view of power as top down, as in Weber's account, and as diffuse and everywhere, as in Foucault's.
- Another tension is between those approaches which see power as having an *external* source, outside its manifestations, as in the economic structure of society in the Marxist account, or as being *produced* by the practices, words and ideas through which it is manifest, as in Foucault's view based on discourse.

Conclusion

This chapter has introduced some of the contemporary debates about consumption, especially the current focus on consumption itself and the idea of a 'consumer society', in order to explore different understandings of this phenomenon. The idea of consumption and the relationship between production and consumption has been used to introduce some of the wider debates within the social sciences about social divisions and inequalities and the operation of power. The contemporary notion that consumption has replaced production as the main influence upon and indicator of social divisions requires further consideration of material differences and other sources of inequality.

The explosion of consumption, in the west especially, and the discussion of its implications have led to the development of different theories, many of which have moved away from the notion that production is the key moment in the process. I have included some discussion of Marxist critiques for two reasons. The first is to provide some of the background to the move from a theory which gives priority to production to theories which provide higher status to consumption. We need to have some idea of what the theories of consumption are challenging and where they come from. Secondly, the Marxist emphasis on the economic base of society and the inequalities that arise from class-based social divisions, provides an important counter argument to the excesses of postmodernism. Marx's analysis necessarily brings in the issue of class divisions and the inequalities that arise from the production process. This critique also highlights some of the constraints upon consumption that are experienced by the less affluent. This approach challenges the postmodernist stress on style and the shift from the material to the representational, but also shows where some of the arguments are coming from.

Consumption cannot be adequately explained through a deterministic view of production and it has been suggested in this chapter that it is not possible to disentangle the processes of production and consumption. Nor is it possible to eliminate the impact of cultural processes from all the moments that are involved in the relationship between production and consumption. The 'turn to culture' in the social sciences has permitted a more extensive exploration of the ways in which meanings are produced, and this is well illustrated in an examination of the phenomenon of the 'consumer society'. As was apparent in the, albeit fictional, example with which this chapter opened, the whole process of exchange is dependent on the meanings as well as the material goods that are consumed. The cultural significance of goods is not a new phenomenon, as Danny Miller argues, but it has assumed greater importance in the contemporary western world because of the intensity and scale of consumption.

Class has received less attention in recent years within the social sciences, but the material base of social divisions still plays an important part and operates along with other sources of inequality. Other analyses of class, which focus more upon market position and the status that can be attached to some social groupings, may have more resonance in the 'consumer society'. The concept of class also invokes the operation of power.

This chapter has briefly mapped out some of the developments and tensions in different approaches to an understanding of power. There has been a move away from a focus upon the sources of power to a concentration upon the mechanisms of power; upon how it works rather than where it comes from. Foucault's work has been important in some branches of the social sciences in offering detailed analyses of the operations of power in myriad ways at multiple different sites. However, although Foucault's insights into the workings of discourses have many applications within this field of consumption, for example in exploring how meanings are produced into which consuming subjects are drawn, his account lacks any possibility of identifying sources of power outside these discourses.

Buying and selling is a vital part of social, economic, cultural and political life and the discussion in this chapter has indicated some of the ways in which the issues arising have been explored within the social sciences. Consumption is much more than going shopping!

Chapter 5

Where do you come from?

Place and race

Introduction

Where do you come from? As was suggested in Chapter 2, this is a question frequently asked when we meet someone for the first time in order to gain some idea of who they are; of their identity. Place, especially the place of origin, is an important part of knowing who we are. Individuals want to know where they were born, where they come from, as well as who their parents are. It may well be that we are trying to gain some understanding of who someone else is by locating them in relation to a particular place. Knowing where someone lives gives us all sorts of clues as to their identity. It is often through place that we position people, not only as individuals, but this is also how governments and official agencies situate us, according to our address or place of birth. Place, especially the place where we were born, or the place where we live, may offer some security in a world which is characterized by mobility and movement, even movement across nations and continents. However, responses to the question 'where do you come from?' may not be so simple. This is the answer given by the athlete Zaf Shah: 'I'm a Bradfordian, a Yorkshireman and I'm British.'

Shah seems quite certain about his identity as British. He is not only British, he is from Yorkshire. As an athlete competing at a high level one might expect him to represent the UK or England at national level. However, he has applied for dual nationality and prefers to represent Pakistan in international competitive sport. He goes on to say, 'My father fought in the British army, but he came from Kashmir. And I am hungry to show the world that Asians can compete at the highest level and do well' (in Arnot 2002: 2). This is a complicated story. It is not so easy to read off who we are from where we come from, nor is it easy to decide which place is the most important. Different places have different meanings. However Shah's story is a particular story, which links specific places; Kashmir in Pakistan where his father came from and Yorkshire, the particular region in which Bradford, the town in the UK where he lives, is situated. Shah offers a specific brand of Britishness that has different strands. Indeed, he is suggesting that he wants to retain his identity in relation to his parents' country of origin. Shah was a promising cricketer in his teens but, in spite of being praised at the highest levels, was not selected to play for his home county cricket club, Yorkshire. His experience of rejection is described by Chris Arnot as 'tasting the bitterness that many British-born Asian sportsmen and women have felt before' (ibid.: 2). Shah changed his sport and did achieve considerable success. What is not stated explicitly in this story is the power relations of empire and of a colonial past that are part of the story of who Shah is. There is the implication in Arnott's account that not being selected to play cricket for his county might have been the result of some kind of racialized prejudice.

It may be for a political reason, that is he wants to show that athletes from Kashmir can be successful at the highest levels, that Shah chooses dual nationality and to compete as an athlete for Pakistan and not for England, even though he sees himself as British. Place is deeply implicated in people's histories and the routes which they, their families and the people with whom they identify, have travelled.

Why is place important? In this chapter I want to suggest that it is important for two main reasons. Firstly, place matters because it locates people. Place provides us with an identity that is associated with not only the place where they currently live, but the different places with which they have been associated. This is especially important at a time in history when there is large-scale movement of people across the globe, whether for economic or political and social reasons. Place can offer some sense of security, either in relation to the place which has been left, perhaps the 'real', 'true' home, or the place where people currently live and which perhaps provides safety from a place where there was considerable danger, as in the case of asylum seekers. Place can provide a sense of belonging. Secondly, place, especially the place where we live, provides insight into the ways in which the society is ordered and organized. The places where we live provide information about who we are, how we live.

Summary

- Place is important in shaping experience and social relations.
- We know ourselves through the place we live and the place we come from.
- Others place us in relation to our home and where we come from.

Roots and routes

Increasingly more and more people have different places associated with their own biographies. The movement of people across the globe is not, of course, a new phenomenon, but through the twentieth and into the twenty-first centuries, there has been extensive migration, resulting from war, economic and environmental disasters, the movement of markets and the overall impact of globalization. People move across countries and continents, as well as within their own country of birth, *Extensive migration*

for a whole range of reasons including the need to find employment. In such *harder to*

circumstances it becomes more difficult to fix one place as being of primary *put*

importance. In such times it may be more useful to look at the different places that *place as*

are associated with people and the routes that they have travelled, rather than fixing *significant.*

one place as the source of who they are, their roots.

The artistic director of Britain's oldest Asian theatre company Jatinder Verma, asked about his 2002 epic production of the play *Journey to the West*, the story of the migration of Asian people from East Africa in 1968 and their settlement in the UK, 'Is your play about roots?' He replied,

> It depends how you're spelling the word . . . I prefer to think of it as r-o-u-t-e-s. Roots lead backwards. Routes are more progressive, leading you to make connections with others. I'm not interested in the particular village in India where my grandfather came from. My identity is located on the road. East Africans are a real conundrum for modern anthropologists because, in some ways, we represent the future, beyond ethnicity. In a truer sense, we are world citizens. I know people who are moving on again, to America. It's as if, having taken the first step out of India, our people are perpetually on the move.
>
> (in Arnot 2002)

Verma cites the specific example of East African Asian people and, in this very short quotation, conjures up ideas of movement and routes. 'My identity is located on the road', he says. His own autobiography embodies movement. He arrived in the UK from Kenya aged 14, his own family of origin having travelled from India to East Africa years before. Verma's *Journey to the West* includes three plays, which mirror the routes he and his family have travelled. The first is set in 1901 following the first exodus from Gujerat, which began in the late nineteenth century. The second is set in 1968 and the third in the present in the twenty-first century. Verma's story is one of success and the routes that he has traversed, which make up his identity.

What does Verma mean by routes? How does this distinction between roots and routes work? The routes he talks about involve the journeys he has taken, the paths which he and other diasporic people have followed and the narratives in which they have been involved. Routes link journeys and stories, places and people. Verma's preference for routes rather than roots also attributes more mobility and more potential for change and adaptation to routes. Routes are dynamic. As he says people who have already travelled from India to East Africa to the UK might travel elsewhere and create new opportunities and new identities. In this account routes seem to afford more potential for agency and for people taking some control over their own lives. It is this potential for change and the desire to look forward as well as backwards that Verma clearly finds attractive and which makes 'routes a better description than "roots"'. However, the routes he has travelled also relate to his past and provide the inspiration for the plays that he has written. These come from past experience, from the experience of *diaspora* but particularly from the journeys which he has travelled, the routes he has already taken. This is what informs the question to which his response is that he prefers routes to roots. Diaspora involves the dispersal of people across the globe. The term was first used to describe the movement and resettling of Jewish people around the world, but it is now used very widely to describe the identities of a range of people in the contemporary globalized world.

Roots tell us about where we have come from; roots are very much involved with the past and with myths of origin. This is not to suggest that a myth is a distortion of truth or a falsehood, but rather – in the sense that Roland Barthes has understood myth – as the means through which we make sense of our lives. Barthes has been well known for his analyses of what he calls the mythologies of popular culture, fashion, advertising, sport, the mass media, which transform culture into what appears to be universal, even 'natural' (1972). Barthes' understanding of myth is not that it distorts or hides the truth but that myths are what are taken as true in any particular culture. Myths are like the stories we each tell ourselves in order to make sense of who we are. Similarly, groups, communities and nations tell themselves collective stories about their identities. A myth is thus a way of making sense of the world through 'a complex system of beliefs which a society constructs in order to sustain and authenticate its own sense of being: i.e. the very fabric of its system of meaning' (Hawkes 1988: 131). Barthes saw myths as operating in contemporary culture so that they appeared to be quite natural, by covering over the contradictions thus making them seem 'normal'.

In this sense a myth becomes absorbed into culture – taken for granted – and merges with nature. It is clear that Verma has more interest and investment in the dynamics of the present and the future, and the possibilities for change than in tracing his past and his origins in an Indian village, but roots cannot be easily dismissed.

As Madan Sarup suggests 'It is important to know where we come from. All people construct a home, all people have a place to which they feel an attachment, a belongingness. This is in contrast to some postmodernist writers who stress the subject as a nomad, a wanderer, roaming from place to place. We have to understand the power and pull of home' (1996: 181). Whilst movement, change and the possibilities of the new might be attractive, there is also the idea of belonging, of home and of some authentic source of certainty that also has appeal both for individuals and for ethnic groups and nations.

In Chapter 2, I suggested that individuals often seek the security of a named 'true' parentage that confirms the ties of kinship. We want to know who our real and genetic parents are in order to know who we are. So too do collectivities of people, whether in ethnic groups or nations. Journeys that are taken so often involve home, whether it is home as the starting point, to which origins can be traced, or home as the desired point of return. Home is associated with sanctuary and security and may carry the romanticized myth of return, even when it is push factors that have led to exile in the first place. People need a sense of place and of belonging and this is often translated into the desire for roots and some sense of authentic origins, a start to the story so that we can move forward through having laid claim to a myth of origin. The question is whether the idea of roots and the emphasis on a single place can deliver the security and feeling of belonging that people may seem to want. Verma acknowledges the pull of India for East African Asian people like himself. Even though he has never lived in India, his birthplace being in Nairobi, which was where he lived until he was 14, he understands the notion of calling India 'home' even though it is a place where he has only ever been a visitor. In his view the conceptualization of India as 'home' belongs very much in the imaginary. Verma's idea of 'home' is like Benedict Anderson's (1983) notion that belonging to a nation, having a national identity, means being part of an 'imagined community'. Verma's views indicate the importance of place, but more particularly places and the routes we have travelled, rather than stressing the priority of roots and a single place.

Summary

- Place can be part of a myth of origin, where we seek our roots.
- Most people do not belong only in one place, so the idea of routes is more useful than roots.
- Routes cover the places we are and have been associated with.
- Routes allow for association with new places; they are dynamic and allow for change.

Place

> Identity is connected to a particular place . . . by a feeling that you belong to that place. It's a place in which you feel comfortable, or at home, because part of how you define yourself is symbolized by certain qualities of that place.
>
> (Rose 1990: 89)

Place is important in shaping our sense of who we are. Place also plays a significant part in shaping our life chances; place is where our life is influenced by an interaction between social and economic factors, social divisions and to a greater or lesser extent the levels of choice we may be able to exercise in the matter.

ACTIVITY

Stop for a moment and think about where you live. What factors have influenced this aspect of your life? Did you have any choice? Would you prefer to live somewhere else if you did have more choice?

COMMENT

There are a whole range of factors which you might cite. Where you live might be determined by family circumstances, by your job, your culture or ethnicity and your resources. You may feel you belong in a particular place, with family, friends and those who share your ethnicity. You may have been attracted to life in the city or the countryside and have made a conscious choice or you may have moved because of your partner's work. All sorts of factors are relevant but they are likely to come into the categories of class, gender and ethnicity along with generation, physical accessibility and access to facilities, sexuality and culture. Access to resources is a key factor in enabling us to exercise choice, and choice is likely to be exercised in different ways at different points in the life cycle.

Place gives meaning to and shapes social inequalities. The place where you live is important in influencing your life chances. The term 'life chances' was used by the sociologist Max Weber in his analysis of social class and status. For example the ownership of property and goods determine a person's chances of realizing their goals in society. The expression has since passed into more general use in the social sciences in relation to social mobility and equal opportunities, as mentioned in Chapter 1 in the context of education.

Place may reflect social divisions but it also constructs and shapes those divisions. Where you live can have a major impact upon your life chances. Places are not simply geographical locations; the people who live there shape the places and the places influence the lives of those who inhabit them. Place may be important but there is not a simple equation between where you live and who you are. We may accord different status and weighting to different places at different times. It is also the case that others position us in relation to our understanding of place. Place can carry a complicated and even contradictory set of meanings.

The English writer Tony Parker went to Belfast in Northern Ireland in 1991 to conduct a series of interviews with different local people. Belfast is a city where place and culture, identity and nation are defining features of everyday life especially in relation to politics and religion. As Parker observed: 'The first thing you need to know about someone as soon as you meet them – and they equally need to know about you – is whether each or both of you is Protestant or Catholic. To be "neither" is not sufficient' (Parker 1994: 3). He goes on to illustrate how closely these identities are linked to place. He cites different examples including going into an estate agent's to enquire about a property. It appears that the estate agent assumes that Parker is a Protestant, being English, but he attempts to find out, just to make sure. The estate agent mentions the Malone Road, an area that was formerly largely Protestant but which had in recent years become mostly Catholic, to see what Parker's response would be. Lacking the specific knowledge of place that is required to pick up the clue Parker does no more than ask about the housing on this road. The estate agent is endeavouring to find out about Parker's identity by using clues which Parker fails to read accurately. This is how we understand others and make ourselves known to them, but sometimes we lack the detailed knowledge to read the clues correctly.

Parker describes going to a chemist's shop in order to get a film processed. The assistant asks him where he would prefer to have the film sent as the shop does not process them on the premises.

> They go either to Johnson and Hunter or Collins and Sullivan, which would you prefer? . . . they both take exactly the same length of time . . . No they're the same price, there's no difference. Johnson and Hunter give you a free fillum with them – but then of course so do Collins and Sullivan too. Well it's for you to say which one you'd like sir. Really no preference? Then we'll send them to Johnson and Hunter. OK?
>
> (Parker 1994: 10)

Parker reflects on this strange situation. If there is no difference between the two companies why does it matter? Why is he asked to choose? As he says:

> Only several weeks later did the penny suddenly drop. Johnson and Hunter are of course at once recognisable merely by their name as being Protestant. Just as Collins and Sullivan are Catholic, as surely as all but the dimmest of the dim would be expected to recognise . . . And of course, because of which she chose, apparently randomly and on reflection most certainly not, it was obvious what she was.
>
> (Parker 1994: 17–18)

Meanings are produced through signs and symbols, names, which are in this instance linked to place. In a place that is as fraught with conflict as Northern Ireland it is not an option to remain neutral. People are expected to take up a position and to understand the codes and clues that are used to position them. Place is closely linked to the ways in which societies are divided. It is not only religion and culture which divide up communities by the places in which people live. In other situations the estate agent's strongest consideration would be whether the client had the resources to buy or rent a house in a particular place. The place where you live is closely connected to a whole range of life chances.

Place and postcodes

What do we mean by place? Place is a geographical location but it carries other meanings as well. The place where you live has different meanings. It means one thing to the people who live there and may mean other things to those who live elsewhere. As in Tony Parker's experience of Belfast, the different parts of the city mean one thing for those for whom that location is home and another for those who live in a different community. Place may be home to one group and a hostile and dangerous place for other people who live outside that place. Place carries political meanings but also meanings associated with consumption and the purchase of a whole range of goods and services. Place can be categorized according to politics, class, culture and ethnicity. There are different reasons for classifying places and for classifying people by the places in which they live. The health service needs evidence of the concentration of people who might be suffering particular forms of ill health and disease. Governments require data on areas of high unemployment. Neighbourhoods are categorized according to educational achievement and how many young people carry on to higher education, for example by the Department for Education and Employment and by the Higher Education Funding Council. All of these associations between people and places are linked to the policy requirements of the state but the associations go further. Public policies and state interventions are also based on assumptions about the links between particular people, places and culture, which themselves contribute to the further classification of a place as deprived or problematic. Carrying such a label may lead to additional resource allocation but it also creates meanings about a place and may make it difficult for those who live there to redefine themselves. For example local authorities deploy Census and other sources of official data to link places and social problems, such as crime and deviancy. The Social Exclusion Unit was established by the Labour government in 1997 in order to target places associated with social deprivation. This association of place with social exclusion and disadvantage also reflects the ways in which countries can be divided geographically and socially, with a higher concentration of poverty and inequality being experienced in specific geographical areas as in the UK example of the 'north/south divide'.

Place is increasingly seen as concerned with lifestyle. The above examples outline lifestyles that may be associated with risk and a higher incidence of social deprivation, but there are also those places associated with social advantage and with affluence. These meanings attached to place have become increasingly important in recent times. Over the last two decades of the twentieth century, marketing and promotional techniques were developed using systems of targeting potential customers in particular areas. This is

> based on the idea that birds of a feather flock together, it gives recognition to the fact that people with broadly similar economic, social and lifestyle characteristics tend to congregate in particular neighbourhoods and exhibit similar patterns of purchasing behaviour and outlook.
>
> (Wilson *et al*. 1992: 202)

This kind of approach which classifies communities according to lifestyle, culture and, especially, what the people who live in them buy, represents a move away from a class-based analysis of social divisions. Instead of class-based measures of social divisions, the Henley Centre, one of Britain's leading management consultancies, argues that the most effective method of classifying people is to identify the drivers of a particular market's demand. This is followed by categorizing consumers along lines based largely on where people live (The Henley Centre 2000).

Postcode classifications offer descriptions of a particular postcode zone giving information such as:

Demographics   the age profile
Socio-economic profile   occupations, employment
Housing   owner-occupied, rented, council, size of houses
Food and drink   type of food and drink consumed, fresh, frozen, tinned foods, prepared meals, fruit, alcohol
Durables   car ownership and that of 'brown' (televisions, videos, DVDs) and 'white' (washing machines, dishwashers) consumer goods
Finance   earnings, savings, credit cards
Media   newspapers, TV and radio
Leisure   holidays, sport
Attitudes   towards gender roles, leisure activities and media.

These categories are drawn from those using systems such as those of ACORN (A Classification of Residential Neighbourhoods), which are used by companies who seek to target their direct mailings in order to ensure maximum take-up of their goods. When you collect your mail in the morning you may be surprised at the amount of 'junk mail' but, unless you have specifically requested the material it is very likely that you have been sent this mail because of your postcode.

This use of place, specifically as measured and classified by postcode, focuses on lifestyle. Whilst the word has been used in the past in the social sciences, for example in sociology in Max Weber's work on social class and status, it has recently become more widely used. As the sociologist Mike Featherstone argues:

> Within contemporary consumer culture it connotes individuality, self-expression and a stylistic self-consciousness. One's body, clothes, speech, leisure pastimes, eating and drinking preference, home, car, choice of holidays, etc. are to be regarded as indicators of individuality of taste and sense of style of the owner/consumer. In contrast to the designation of the 1950s as an era of grey conformism, a time of *mass* consumption, changes in production techniques, market segmentation and consumer demand for a wider range of products, are often regarded as making possible a greater choice (the management of which itself becomes an art form) not only for youth of the post 1960s generation, but increasingly for the middle aged and the elderly.
>
> (Featherstone 1991: 83)

It looks as if we are all involved; even the elderly are expected to look cool and buy into 'lifestyle'. Stop and think about Featherstone's account of lifestyle. He emphasizes choice and the agency that consumers are able to exercise. This counters some of the points made earlier about the association between place and social divisions. People are classified by the place in which they live, for example as socially deprived, without exercising any choice in the matter. What do you think might be missing in Featherstone's account?

Those who have been forced to live in postcode areas that are classified as socially deprived, because they lack the resources to live anywhere else, are unlikely to be targeted by advertising and promotional material. They are also unlikely to be able to define themselves as they might want in relation to clothes, cars and other patterns of consumption.

Pierre Bourdieu (1986) used the concept of cultural capital to explain the complex ways in which socio-economic class and lifestyle interact. For Bourdieu, social divisions cannot be based entirely on economic relations of power. Other elements have to be considered. Bourdieu identified four forms of capital: economic, social, cultural and symbolic. Beverley Skeggs summarizes these four forms as follows:

i. *economic capital:* this includes income, wealth, inheritance and financial assets

ii. *social capital:* capital generated through relationships with others, links with influential groups

iii. *cultural capital:* this can exist in three forms – in an embodied state, that is in the form of long-lasting dispositions of the mind and body; in the objectified state, in the form of cultural goods; and in the institutionalized state, resulting in such as educational qualifications . . .

iv. *symbolic capital*: this is the form the different types of capital take once they are perceived as recognized and legitimate. Legitimation is the key mechanism in the conversion of power. Cultural capital has to be legitimated before it can have symbolic power. Capital has to be regarded as legitimate before it can be capitalized upon.

(Skeggs 1997: 7)

Economic power does not necessarily guarantee what Bourdieu calls 'distinction'. Just being rich does not ensure that someone is accepted in all social circles, even if they can afford to buy a house in a very expensive area where those in the highest social circles live. In contemporary life it seems that the economic and cultural capital of football stars and those of popular culture have been legitimated but this was not always the case. Those who live in the poorest areas are likely to lack all four forms of capital, although as Bourdieu argues, certain forms of cultural capital may be available. For example in impoverished areas it may be possible to access cultural capital through engaging in certain sports like boxing (Plate 5.1).

Summary

- Place shapes and reflects and reproduces life chances.
- Place is linked to lifestyle, for example in the targeting of companies seeking new markets for their products.
- Postcodes can also signify social deprivation, which can be used both to label certain places and to target support and welfare policies and resources.

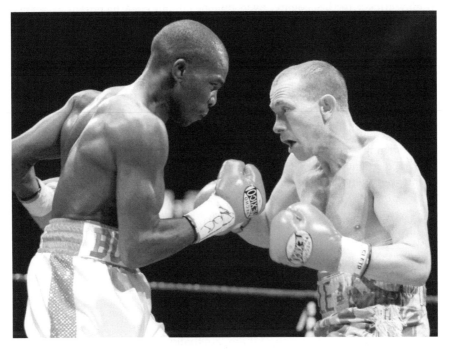

Plate 5.1 Cultural capital: getting physical
Source: © EMPICS Sports Photography.

Place and race

Place and *race* are connected. Think back to the example at the start of this chapter. The athlete Zaf Shah's family had lived in different places. They had moved to the UK, along with many other people from British colonial countries, after the Second World War. In the period following the war and the passing of the 1948 British Nationality Act, there was a significant increase in the numbers of people moving to the UK from countries of the New Commonwealth, although subsequent legislation in the 1960s and 1970s curtailed this trend. What has this got to do with race? Race is a problematic term and we will think about how it is used and the different meanings that it carries in this section. Many social scientists prefer the word *ethnicity*. Shah's experience can be used to illustrate some of the ways in which race and place intersect, which can be deployed to introduce a fuller consideration of what we mean by race. You will recall that Shah, whilst seeing himself as British, wanted to compete at international levels representing Pakistan, the country his parents had left to come to settle in England. One of the reasons suggested for Shah's enthusiasm for representing Pakistan rather than England, was his previous experience of rejection in his home county. He was not selected to play cricket for his county, even though he had been identified as a very promising young player. This was in a county with a relatively high proportion of people from Pakistan and India. The underlying message of Arnot's discussion above is that Shah's rejection was caused by *racist* attitudes, and that these racist attitudes were connected with place, the places Shah's family had come from, and with visible difference.

Thinking about the words we use

I have already used several different terms in order to address some of the issues here, race, ethnicity and racism. Sometimes social scientists use other terms in order to overcome some of the problems involved.

ACTIVITY

Take these three words and jot down what you associate with each:

Race
Ethnicity (or *ethnic*)
Racism

Think of an example for each of them, a situation in which you may say one of these words. In everyday use you might be more likely to use 'ethnic' than ethnicity, but you can choose either.

COMMENT

You might have thought of several different examples. These are words around which there may be some anxiety. Sometimes we are not sure which word to use. Should we talk about race or is ethnicity more appropriate and acceptable? Race is sometimes used to suggest some kind of biological categorization that differentiates the human species, based on the idea that human beings can be classified into racial groups. You may have thought of examples in everyday discourse or in the media where race is used to describe black or south Asian people, as in 'race riots' in inner-city areas. Race is a term with a wide range of meanings. It may invoke biology, or be about visible difference or be a catch-all expression to cover a range of differences among human beings. Ethnicity might be less in everyday use than 'ethnic', which often refers to certain kinds of food, clothes or music which are seen as outside the mainstream, belonging to 'other' cultures, perhaps even connoting some kind of exotic characteristics. For example, Indian food may be called 'ethnic', whereas British fish and chips, or even McDonald's, would not. Sometimes people use the term ethnic only to refer to people who are different from themselves, and especially to refer to non-white people and cultures, as if white people did not have an ethnicity. As the Parekh Report points out:

There is a gulf between specialist and non-specialist usage of the term 'ethnic'
... In popular usage the term 'ethnic' implies non-western (as in 'ethnic
food'), non-classical (as in 'ethnic music'), non-white ('ethnic communities')
or non-British (as in the late 1990s dispute about insignia on British Airways
aircraft).

(Parekh 2000a: xxiii)

Racism is more clearly understood as discrimination against people who belong
to an identifiable group on unfair grounds. You may have thought of examples of
situations where you have experienced racism, either against yourself or observing
incidences or perhaps having read about them in the press. These are mostly
common-sense everyday ways of understanding and using these terms. Language
is very important in producing meanings through which we make sense of the world
and the words we use matter. This is particularly apparent in discourses of race,
ethnicity and racism and is well illustrated in everyday experience. What light can
the further explorations of social science throw on these terms and how might they
be understood as concepts in a deeper study of the society in which we live?

Race

Kum-Kum Bhavnani suggests this definition of race:

'Race' is a concept which has no biological basis ... All the criteria which
apparently assert the reality of 'race', such as hair type, shape of face, blood
group, are shown not to be discrete across human populations and genepools.
In other words we are all members of the same species ... However, the
acceptance of 'race' as a scientifically valid concept has helped to create a
certain type of legitimation for racism: that is, that racism comes to be seen
as 'natural' and as intrinsic to 'human nature'. Given that there is no sound
evidence from the natural and biological sciences to justify the supposition
that the human species can be divided up into separate 'races', however, both
'race' and racism become economic, political, ideological and social
expressions. In sum 'race' is not a biological category which is empirically
defined. Rather, it is created and reproduced, as well as being challenged and
eliminated through economic, political and ideological institutions.

(Bhavnani 1993: 31–2)

What sort of definition of race is being offered here? You will notice that Bhavnani
uses 'race' in inverted commas. This is a common practice in the social sciences,
in order to differentiate between the use of race as a biological classificatory system,
a view now largely discredited, and the use the term has for describing and
ultimately explaining social divisions and conflicts based on this aspect of
difference. How does Bhavnani define 'race'? What are the key points?

- Race is not a biological category. There is no scientific evidence for this view, but it has been very influential in the past and informs contemporary views, especially those leading to racism.
- Racial divisions seem natural because they are so much part of everyday life; they are constantly represented and reproduced, for example through the media.
- Racial categories and 'race' is often based on the visible differences, such as hair type and skin colour, among people.
- The emphasis here is on the social construction of 'race'. 'Race' and racism are social structures. They may constrain people but there is resistance and people can exercise agency and reject racism.

The main argument here seems to be to focus on the social construction of 'race', whilst acknowledging physical characteristics and differences between people, to argue that what is really important is not the differences themselves but the meanings that different societies attribute to them. These meanings often involve hierarchies and hostility, which is where racism is involved.

The Parekh Report argues that the term race is crucially important since it:

> Refers to the reality of racism. It is unhelpful, however, to the extent that it reflects and perpetuates the belief that the human species consists of separate races. A further disadvantage is that overuse can deflect attention from culture and religious aspects of racism as distinct from those that are concerned with physical appearance. It needs often, therefore, to be complemented with other terms.
>
> This report uses the phrase 'race equality and cultural diversity', sometimes shortened to 'race and diversity', to refer to its overall area of concern. The phrase stresses that addressing racism requires not only the creation of equality but also the recognition of difference . . .
>
> The term 'racist violence' is preferred to 'racial violence', as recommended by the Stephen Lawrence Inquiry report. It alludes to the causes of such violence and to how perpetuators justify it.
>
> (Parekh 2000a: xxiv)

Ethnicity

Ethnicity is a term which includes some sharing of culture, possibly language and place. This place could be the place you come from or the place where you live. According to Avtah Brah, ethnicity and especially ethnic identities are maintained through

> A belief in common ancestry, claims to a shared history that gives shape to feelings of shared struggles and shared destinies, attachment to a homeland

which may or may not coincide with the place of residence, and a sense of belonging to a group with a shared language, religion, social customs and traditions.

(Brah 1993: 15)

Some social scientists have adopted the use of ethnicity in preference to 'race' because of the associations of 'race' with racists, biological categories that have involved the assertion of the superiority of some races over others. Although others have pointed out that ethnicity lacks a political dimension. For example, Bhikhu Parekh points out that, counter to the common-sense understanding of 'ethnic' as involving non-white or non-western cultures, there is a more precise description of ethnicity: 'For specialists, an ethnic group is one whose members have common origins, a shared sense of history, a shared culture and a sense of collective identity. All human beings belong to an ethnic group in this sense' (Parekh 2000a: xxi). However, because of the risk of misunderstanding – the common-sense assumptions about ethnicity as a synonym for 'non-white' or 'non-western' – the term 'ethnic' can be problematic. It also does not address the political meanings of hierarchies of ethnic groups, for example the racism that is often implicated in attributing ethnicity. Whilst it is indeed the case that all human beings belong to some kind of ethnic group, using this term in all cases might obscure or marginalize the discrimination which is directed at some groups more than others.

However, ethnic is the term largely used in official statistics, for example in the census in order to classify populations. You can probably think of several other situations in which you are asked to disclose your own ethnic identity, for example in job applications, where ethnic monitoring is a requirement of equal opportunities and diversity policies. Finding the right words is difficult and complicated and beset by problems, but this is not only a matter of getting the right word. The words we use, not only carry existing meanings, they also create new meanings. It has been a very important aspect of what has been called 'identity politics', to use terminology that frees people from the negative associations of some of the terms used in the past. Ethnic has been used in the context of equal opportunities policies and practices in order to avoid the limitations of 'race' as involving biological categories. You may think of other examples, such as the use of 'disabled people' rather than the derogatory 'handicapped', or 'gay' as a positive, celebratory alternative to the clinical category of homosexuality. Words, along with other features of representational systems, images, practices and rituals, are important in shaping and constructing how we understand the world, and as part of political activity.

An associated term often accompanying references to ethnicity is 'minority'. You are very likely to have seen references to 'ethnic minorities' in media reports and on television programmes, especially providing news coverage or drawing on the data of official statistics. Less frequently do we see or hear references to the 'ethnic majority', although a majority always haunts discussion of minorities. Although the expression 'ethnic minority', or sometimes used the other way round as 'minority ethnic', is in common usage, it too is problematic. As Parekh comments

> The term 'minority' has connotations of 'less important' or 'marginal'. In many settings it is not only insulting but also mathematically misleading or inaccurate. Furthermore it perpetuates the myth of white homogeneity – the notion that everyone who does not belong to a minority is by that token a member of a majority, in which there are no significant differences or tensions.
>
> (Parekh 2000a: xxiii)

The claim of homogeneity applies to whiteness too. The argument here suggests that 'white' is a single category with shared ethnicity, which it clearly is not. Different groups of white people have different histories, cultures, religion and languages and adopt different positions in relation to others.

One of the routes through which meanings are produced about whiteness is through classificatory systems such as the categories to classify persons in a variety of places. The census offers one example of a site at which people are recorded as belonging to particular ethnic categories. Censuses provide a means of racial categorization. Policy decisions are made on the bases of census data. Although people may be invited to categorize themselves, the categories provided are determined by others, by those who design the questions. The census does not just classify race, it also decides what counts. For example, Sharon Lee (1993), using the US census, has demonstrated that census categories have suggested that any proportion of 'black', 10 per cent, 20 per cent makes the person black, rather than 90 per cent or 80 per cent white. Census categories have altered in recent years, although categories of non-white people have changed more than those of white people, with changing times. In the case of the US census, some categories remained constant, notably that of 'white' at the top of the list for two hundred years, since 1850 in fact. The US census changed to include Irish as whites whereas they had previously been categorized as 'black' (Warren and Twine 1997). In the early nineteenth century Celts and other European migrants were classified as 'black' in the United States but all, along with the Irish, became white by the end of the nineteenth century. Categories may be used for political purposes, for example 'black' may be used as a political category, whereas white can be seen as an assumed class without differences. In the 2001 UK census a question on religion was introduced to ascertain more information about the diversity of respondents in the 'Asian' category. However, there have been those who bear the visible difference of whiteness yet who are not classified as white. This has been the case with the Irish, who have been a key 'other' for the British. The Irish have been racialized even more than the Welsh and negatively characterized by particular stereotypical features. Roddy Doyle in his novel and film, *The Commitments*, has a character claim that the 'Irish are the blacks of Europe'. At different times people are differently classified and there may be 'degrees of whiteness'.

Racism

What do we mean by racism? What sort of acts, thoughts, representations and practices might be so labelled? Here are some examples from the Parekh Report.

> He swore and shouted 'Paki', something I'm used to being called. I felt that the incident wasn't significant enough to report. In fact the police would have laughed at me.
>
> Two of us went shopping together, always. Two of us had to be in the house to defend the others. We used to be scared going home. We used to phone Mum and say, 'Mum, I am coming round the corner. Please look out of the window.' We had to let the family know what shops we were going to so if we were late they could go and check. Everything was really organised.
>
> I still don't feel British. Because I know we haven't been fully accepted. We still walk down the street and get called a Paki.
>
> (Parekh 2000a: 58)

Many of the voices recorded in the Parekh Report speak of daily acts of racism and xenophobia, of conducting their daily routines in an atmosphere of discrimination and hostility, often taking place on the street and perpetrated by the most disadvantaged of white youths. These acts constitute some of the most explicit experiences of racism, ranging in seriousness from name-calling to actual acts of violence. Such acts are, of course, against the law, but still take place. Racism also has a less direct and less immediately obvious face, which nonetheless has enormous impact upon people's lives. It can be seen as operating in education, in employment, in the provision of welfare services and even in the criminal justice system.

The Macpherson Report (1999) on the murder of the black, UK teenager Stephen Lawrence gave much more public awareness to the concept *institutional racism*. Hitherto this concept had been largely confined to academic research within the social sciences, but Sir William Macpherson put the expression into everyday usage. His report noted that, although directly racist practices had been prohibited by anti-racist legislation like the Race Relations Act and by the implementation of a range of anti-discriminatory policies, for example in education and by employers in the public and private sectors of employment, racism was still present. The only difference was that it was practised *implicitly* in the procedures and policies of many public bodies. The report's statement has been widely quoted as a definition, although Macpherson's claim was that it should provoke further discussion and not be fixed for all time. The suggested explanation was that institutional racism involved the collective failure of an organization or institution to provide appropriate and professional service and to permit unwitting prejudice, ignorance, thoughtlessness and racist stereotyping (in Parekh 2000a: 70). The Macpherson Report suggested that

The term institutional racism should be understood to refer to the way institutions may systematically treat or tend to treat people differently in respect of race. The addition of the word 'institutional' therefore identifies the source of the differential treatment; this lies in some sense within the organisation rather than simply with the individuals who represent it. The production of differential treatment is 'institutionalised' in the way the organisation operates.

(Macpherson 1999, Para 2.2)

This concept of institutionalized racism has been criticized in many ways but it is important for a number of reasons. Firstly, it points to the ways in which racism is socially produced and reinforced; racism is a social structure, rather than being the responsibility of individual agents and the outcome of individual acts. If it is embedded in social institutions this suggests targets and strategies for change, rather than punishing individuals only. Everyone is implicated and we all have a responsibility. Secondly, the concept draws upon empirical and theoretical work within the social sciences and illustrates the relationship between social science and policy. This is not only important for social scientists! It indicates the ways in which academic work supports policy making and permits the application of the findings of sustained endeavour, linking intellectual, academic work and other areas of work within the wider society. Social scientists do not live in ivory towers!

Race and gender

Another of the interconnections that it is important to suggest in exploring the impact of race, ethnicity and racism, is that between race and gender. As we saw in Chapter 2, people have multiple identities. Everyone has some kind of ethnic identity along with a gender identity, and others relate to work, family, friendships, sexuality, being able-bodied or having some disability and to nation. Race and ethnicity do not exist in isolation from other areas of human experience. This is well demonstrated by a speech made in 1851 by Sojourner Truth, a woman who was born into slavery in the United States. She campaigned for both the abolition of slavery and for equal rights for women.

Well, children, where there is so much racket, there must be something out of kilter, I think between the Negroes of the South and the women of the North – all talking about rights – the white men will be in a fix pretty soon. But what's all this talking about? That man over there says that women need to be helped into carriages, and lifted over ditches, and to have the best place everywhere. Nobody helps me any best place. And ain't I a woman? Look at me! Look at my arm. I have plowed (sic), I have planted and I have gathered into barns. And no man could head me. And ain't I a woman? I could work as much, and eat as much as any man – when I could get it – and bear the lash as well! And ain't I a woman? I have born children and seen most of them sold into slavery, and when I cried out with a mother's grief, none but Jesus heard me. And ain't I a woman?

(in Bhavnani and Coulson 1986: 83)

Truth points out most forcefully in this powerful speech that she is no less a woman because she belongs to a group of people who are oppressed on grounds of race too. It is the legacy of slavery and of colonialism that has informed the development of black feminist approaches to social divisions and inequality. Such critiques have stressed the need to look at the ways in which gender and race operate together in shaping experience. Black feminists have argued that feminist politics needs to take on board the specific experiences of different women, rather than assuming that there is a single category 'woman' with shared history and shared experiences of oppression. There are differences in culture, in family, in religion, in place and in history, all of which make for particular experiences, about which it is not possible to generalize on the basis of gender. For example, whereas the women's movement in the west has argued strongly for free access to contraception and abortion in order to control their fertility, for many black women control of their fertility would have a different emphasis. They would stress the need to be able to have children and in some instances to have access to fertility treatment, which has on occasion been denied. Race, class and gender are all significant influences and operate together. Not only do we need to acknowledge all these different factors, but we also need to include specific circumstances and histories.

Race and nation

There are times when race is also widely enmeshed with the experience of nation. For example at the beginning of this chapter we considered the question of how being black, or more specifically south Asian, and British, is possible. The experience of racism can militate against feelings of inclusion and of being part of the nation where you currently live. One of the examples of the voices quoted in the Parekh Report cited the failure of belonging, saying that he did not feel 'British'.

What we mean by Britain and 'the British people' is, however, deeply problematical. Most modern nations consist of diverse and disparate people. 'The British people' is the result of a series of conquests – Celtic, Roman, Saxon, Viking and Norman. The UK presents a mixture of peoples and a mix of cultures. There are issues of naming involved too. Britain usually refers to England, Scotland and Wales, whereas the UK includes these three and Northern Ireland.

What do we mean by a nation? For example in the UK, which is a nation state, England, Scotland and Wales are usually thought of as nations. Some people would consider Ireland, the whole land mass and its people a nation, whereas others, notably Ulster Protestants would strongly contest this. Nation is a contested term. Nation states have external, fixed demarcated borders and some uniformity of law that is recognized as such. A nation has a named people who recognize their shared identity which is the outcome of a shared history, culture and of belonging to a homeland. In this context we are focusing on the idea of a nation and the question of how race and nation interconnect. The nation is also a cultural community and brings together the political nation state and the culture of the nation. Does having a national culture mean that there is a unified culture? There may indeed be a tendency to attempt to achieve some sort of unity. It may be that this unity excludes those who feel excluded, like some of the people whose views were expressed in the Parekh Report. The anthropologist and philosopher Ernest Gellner argues that all modern societies require the development of a common culture and language or they will disintegrate. As he argues,

> culture is now the necessary shared medium, the life-blood, or perhaps rather the minimal shared atmosphere, within which alone the members of the society can breathe and survive and produce. For a given society it must be one in which they can all breathe and speak and produce; so it must be the same culture.
>
> (Gellner 1983: 37–8)

This view seems to undermine the notion of an inclusive national culture which encompasses diversity and embraces differences among its people. It does foreground the importance of culture and the combination of the political and cultural aspects of nation, which are useful for exploring some of the ways in which people may feel that they are excluded as well as the reasons why others feel that they belong.

The nation as 'imagined community'

The political scientist and historian Benedict Anderson sees the nation as an 'imagined community':

> It is imagined because the members of even the smallest nation will never know most of their fellow members, meet them, or even hear of them . . . The nation is imagined as limited because even the largest of them, encompassing perhaps a billion living human beings, has finite, if elastic, boundaries beyond which lie other nations . . . it is imagined as a community, because, regardless of actual inequality and exploitation that may prevail . . . the nation is always conceived as a deep horizontal comradeship.
>
> (Anderson [1983] 1991: 6–7)

This draws attention to some of the processes that are involved in the construction of nation. How do we imagine ourselves as belonging to a nation? A nation has to be thought of in relation to other nations. We belong to one nation and not to another. According to Anderson, modern nations arose historically from the emergence of new communication media, like printing and the free market activities of capitalist enterprise. New communications systems allowed people to imagine themselves more easily. People are aware of the signifiers of their own nation, the flag, the shared culture and the rituals that are associated with a particular nation. These are the ways in which a nation produces meanings about the culture of nation that is shared.

Rituals

Rituals play a crucial part in sustaining the collective memory and reinstating notions of the nation. Such rituals may have religious and secular aspects. As Emile Durkheim (1915) argued, despite differences in content there are few functional differences between religious, national and secular rituals and ceremonies because their aims and their outcomes are remarkably similar. This has been especially marked in England and Wales, where the monarch is both head of state and head of the Anglican Church and the Church of England in Wales. The established church still plays a significant role in rituals ranging from state events such as the opening of Parliament and state funerals to memorial and commemorative events. Secular occasions such as the Football Association Cup Final even may employ quasi-religious songs and hymns and serve a very similar function in bringing people together for moments of shared national identification. Drawing on the language of religion and the history of the state rituals serve to confirm and establish notions of a British way of life and national identity. Such rituals, especially those that involve the state and its dignitaries as well as the monarch, often draw on historical narratives and the authority of archaic practices, historic costumes and often the use of Latin phrases to lend the status of the past and of past glories to current re-enactments. The military may also be involved. For example, Remembrance Sunday constructs a particular view of belonging to the nation which invokes a military past where the identity of the nation is closely linked to military endeavours and associations of self-sacrifice and heroism. The state funeral provides a site for the enactment of the glorious past of the individual who has died in the context of the nation's past. This was particularly well represented at the funeral of Winston Churchill, the British prime minister during the Second World War, who died in 1965. On this occasion the military had a very dominant presence, and even though this point in time can be seen as marking the end of empire there was a parade of dignitaries and officers of state signifying the past that was. This was a traditional funeral, attended by dignitaries of state, Commonwealth and other world political leaders, the monarchy and the aristocracy. Thousands of people lined the streets, largely deferentially, as British subjects. The funeral of Diana Princess of Wales, in 1997, was in many ways very different. As one observer remarked, people were there as 'British citizens', rather than as British subjects, as at Churchill's funeral (Woodward 2000b). This suggests more active involvement and even control over the shaping of events, rather than being a passive spectator. Diana's funeral saw a break with protocol, the flag at half mast at Buckingham Palace, the Queen responding to the 'people's' demands and the presence of a more diverse range of people, including media stars and Diana's friends. Whereas in 1965, the global presence at Churchill's funeral was that of political leaders, and the largely elderly, white, male colonial order, by 1997 there appeared to be a more diverse, inclusive representation. In 1997, the state ritual involved the expression of emotions and the presence of numerous media stars with the popular singer Elton John singing at the funeral service itself in Westminster Abbey, although many of the traditional rituals of state were maintained (Woodward 2000b). By 1997, the British nation could be seen to have been re-constructed as more diverse, more inclusive with some representation of women and black and Asian British people.

Such rituals offer defining moments in the story of the nation. Through rituals of particular practices, incorporating dignitaries and heroes (even newly constructed popular heroes, as in the case of Diana and her funeral). They retell the nation's history in specific ways that re-present dramatic accounts of national identity, and thus compound people's investment, both in a particular narrative and in a specific story of the nation's 'real', and shared, past.

Another aspect of the process of inclusion and exclusion, which positions people as 'us' and 'them' and more especially insiders and outsiders, is explored in Edward Said's influential work on the western colonialization of Asian societies, *Orientalism* (1978). In this book Said explores the ways in which representations and discourses of colonized peoples as 'Other' and thus as different or inferior, are an integral part of political economic colonialism. His claim is that representational systems in the west produced the idea that the diverse nations of the near and far east can be grouped together as the same, into a single civilization, namely the 'Orient'. Thus the 'Orient' becomes the binary opposite to the west – the 'Occident' – against which the Orient is defined as backward, despotic and undeveloped as well as mysterious and exotic. Said's argument was that the 'Orient' was not discovered but *made*. He argued that 'a very large mass of writers, among them are poets, novelists, philosophers, political theorists, economists and imperial administrators, have accepted the basic distinction between East and West as the starting point for elaborate theories, stories, novels, social descriptions and political accounts concerning the Orient, its people, customs, "mind", destiny and so on' (in Bayoumi and Rubin 2001: 69). In *Orientalism*, Said's aim was to use Michel Foucault's idea of discourse, based on the meanings that are produced through discursive fields, to unpack this whole thought system and to expose its power relations and structures, in order to challenge the dominance of western thought. Said shows how deeply implicated are the practices and representational systems through which such knowledge is produced in the interplay of power between west and east. The identities so produced through these processes are polarized, as are the 'Orient' and the 'Occident'.

How does this connect with race and nation? For example Said's concept of the 'Orient' as 'other' and 'outside' shows how different people within the nation, for example within Britain, are excluded from the culture of the nation. It illustrates not only *who* is excluded, for example peoples who are associated with colonized countries and the 'Orient', but also *how*, for example through the construction of the nation's culture, its rituals, practices and imaginings. Where is race in the imaging and imagining of nationhood and what is the role of race in the shared histories which characterize nations? In countries in the western world such as the UK, the histories that are implicated in the construction of the nation involve some aspect of colonialism. This is at the root of the exclusion of many people from national belonging. Think of the examples that have been cited in this chapter in relation to Britishness. The imagined community may not encompass the full diversity of the nation's history. The stories that are told about 'we British' may be a predominantly white story and exclude the histories of people from Africa, the Caribbean and south Asia, for example.

As Paul Gilroy has argued, in exploring ideas about race and racism and the nation and belonging,

> We increasingly face a racism which avoids being recognised as such because it is able to line up 'race' with nationhood, patriotism and nationalism. A racism which is taken a necessary distance from crude ideas of biological inferiority and superiority now seeks to present an imaginary definition of the nation as a unified *cultural* community. It constructs and defends an image of national culture – homogeneous in its whiteness yet precarious and perpetually vulnerable to attack from enemies within and without . . . This is a racism that answers the social and political turbulence of crisis and crisis management by the recovery of national greatness in the imagination. Its dream-like construction of our sceptered isle as an ethnically purified one provides special comfort against the ravages of [national] decline.
>
> (Gilroy 1992: 87)

However, the contemporary UK is very much a multicultural society in the sense that it includes a wide range of ethnic groups. For example empirical evidence indicates the presence of considerable diversity in the UK population.

Table 5.1 shows that by 2001 about one person in 14 in the UK was from an ethnic minority. The table also indicates the age categories, showing that there is still a relatively low proportion of minority ethnic people in the older age categories. Increasing numbers of people of different ethnicities have led to the claim that the UK is a multicultural society. The evidence would appear to support this in terms of population. However, numbers do not give any clue as to the extent to which minority ethnic people feel that they belong, in the sense of identifying with being British. The continuance of racists acts, including acts of extreme violence as well as the everyday acts of discrimination that minority ethnic people have to suffer, militate against full participation in the multicultural society which the UK might appear to have become. At one level there is a celebration of multicultural Britishness, for example in sport, music and art and even in political life. There are increasing opportunities for the expression of diversity and for full participation in all aspects of contemporary life, including the culture of the nation.

Table 5.1 Population by ethnic group and age, Great Britain, 2000–2001[a]

	Under 16 (%)	16–34 (%)	35–64 (%)	65 and over (%)	All ages (=100%) (millions)
White	20	25	39	16	53.0
Black					
Black Caribbean	23	27	40	10	0.5
Black African	33	35	30	2	0.4
Other Black groups	52	29	17	–	0.3
All Black groups	34	30	31	5	1.3
Indian	23	31	38	7	1.0
Pakistani/Bangladeshi					
Pakistani	36	36	24	4	0.7
Bangladeshi	39	36	21	4	0.3
All Pakistani/Bangladeshi	37	36	23	4	0.9
Other groups					
Chinese	19	38	38	4	0.1
None of the above	32	33	32	3	0.7
All other groups[b]	30	34	33	3	0.8
All ethnic groups[c]	20	26	39	15	57.1

Source: Labour Force Survey, Office for National Statistics.

Notes
a Population living in private households. Combined quarters: spring 2000 to winter 2000–2001.
b Includes those of mixed origin.
c Includes those who did not state their ethnic group.

ACTIVITY

Read this short extract from a speech by the then UK Foreign Secretary Robin Cook, in 2001. The speech assumed some fame – or possibly notoriety – and became known as the 'Tikka Massala' speech.

How does Cook understand Britishness? What makes the nation culturally diverse? How does he see the impact of multiculturalism?

I want to set out our reasons for being optimistic about the future of Britain and Britishness . . . The first element in the debate about the future of Britishness is the changing ethnic composition of the British people themselves. The British are not a race, but a gathering of countless different races and communities, the vast majority of which were not indigenous to these islands . . .

Chicken Tikka Massala is now a true British national dish, not only because it is the most popular, but because it is a perfect illustration of the way Britain absorbs and adapts external influences. Chicken Tikka is an Indian dish. The Massala sauce was added to satisfy the desire of British people to have their meat served in gravy.

(*The Guardian* online 19 April 2001)

COMMENT

This seems a positive reading, although on more detailed investigation we can ask which Britishness is being identified here. Cook's main argument, the one for which this speech became most famous, is that the popularity of a hybrid dish, chicken tikka massala, is proof of genuine cultural and ethnic diversity. It may be evidence of some cultural mixing but his claim is relatively superficial in terms of the complexity and depth of ethnic differences. He still refers to the British adopting the food of 'other' people, but with a starting point which sees Britishness as already existing and others have to be adapted to suit the transforming Britishness, rather than Britishness adapting to the needs and tastes of the ethnic groups which now make up what it means to be British. There is a tension between the new opportunities and diversity of multiculturalism and the constraints of the remnants of racism which still permeate societies such as the UK and impinge upon our understanding of what it means to be British. There are both negative and positive dimensions to this change which is transforming British society and the social sciences in their attempts to comprehend and explain these changes. The social sciences have contributed a questioning approach which leads us to go beyond the statements of politicians or even the everyday practices of our daily lives; to look at the meanings that are attached to these practices. Even the words that we use are subject to deeper investigation and the need to adapt in order to address the demand for greater inclusiveness in what it means to be British.

At different historical moments there may be greater inclusion in national identities expressed through being British or by being English or Welsh or Scottish for minority ethnic people. One of the moments at which we belong to the 'imagined community' of the nation is during sporting competitions at an international level. The men's football World Cup is a good example of a secular coming together of the nation, when huge numbers of English people support the English team. Whilst black players, although not as yet any south Asian players, occupy leading roles in the Premiership and in the England team, racism is still enacted on the terraces and even on the pitch. In the European qualifying rounds in 2002, when England played Slovakia, there were extreme incidences of racism. Emile Heskey and Ashley Cole, two black English players, were subjected to racist taunts as well as there being fighting between fans off the pitch (Plate 5.2). The black players expressed anxiety about playing for their clubs, Liverpool and Arsenal, following this incident. The incidents were greeted with an outcry of disapproval by the English Football Association and there was the claim that England had greatly improved its own record on anti-racism. This illustrates the tension and the trials of moving towards multiculturalism. Racism still exists in

Plate 5.2 Emile Heskey at the European Qualifiers in 2002: racism lives on?
Source: © EMPICS Sports Photography.

the English game as the attempts to eliminate it reveal, through the evidence of campaigns like *Kick Racism Out* and *Football Unites, Racism Divides*. However, on this occasion it seems that the problems were with another nation and England was keen to claim superiority. Maybe a popular mass entertainment activity (albeit largely through spectatorship rather than active participation) like football is one possible avenue towards greater inclusion and the development of anti-racist strategies which could lead to a new multicultural Britishness. Maybe.

Summary

- Race and place are interconnected through past and present experiences.
- Place often means the places we have come from, the routes we have travelled as well as the place where we live.

- Symbolic systems, rituals and language are very important. The language of race creates meanings and has material consequences. Symbols and rituals create inclusion into and exclusion from the culture of the nation.
- Race and gender interrelate and include different and specific experiences of inequalities.
- Race and nation combine to impact upon experience in different ways at different times.

Conclusion

Race and place are interconnected in many ways. Place has different meanings. There is the place where we live and the place where we were born. Place carries meanings related to class and to national and ethnic identity. A study of place and an exploration of the concept of place also raises issues about the degree of agency which people are able to exercise over where they live. Living where we do may be completely outside our own area of choice or we may be in a position to make our own decisions. As with migration between countries, even within the same country there may be push and pull factors and some people are able to exercise much more autonomy than others.

The links between race and place involve the routes that we travel, the places we have lived and, in particular, those places which have the most meaning in shaping our lives. At a time of mass migration these connections are brought to the fore. Of course, migration is not new, but it has intensified over the past century and there are relatively large numbers of people who live in a different place from the one where they were born or where their parents were born. Race is a shorthand expression for a whole range of processes. These include the process of being classified as belonging to a particular race or ethnic group.

It is also important to look at the ways in which race intersects with other aspects of social divisions such as those based on gender and nation. One of the arguments of recent theoretical critiques in the social sciences has been to focus on the ways in which different matters interrelate, rather than seeking to isolate different factors, and in this case different social structures.

These processes can usefully be called *racialization* and *ethnicization*. They look like unnecessarily long words, but they do have the advantage of indicating a process, something that involves change and is ongoing. Race and ethnicity are not fixed, they are constantly being produced. Race is not some biological category fixed and set in our genes. It is a social process that is constantly evolving. One of the major contributions of the social sciences has been first in exploring the empirical evidence about race and place. Secondly, the examination of how race and place are represented and especially the language which we use to present knowledge about race has been an especially important contribution. By asking questions about what we mean by the words we use and the ways in which we construct knowledge about race we are able to reveal some of the power structures which underpin our ideas and practices.

The social sciences have largely stressed the importance of the social, economic, political and cultural production of meanings about race and these are what have been most influential and useful in influencing policies and strategies, in particular to combat the negative impact of racism and to develop new ways of thinking about diversity and difference which can accommodate and welcome change.

Chapter 6

Globalization

All over the place?

Introduction

Globalization has become a familiar term in recent years. It may even have become a commonplace and overused term for a whole range of diverse developments in politics, economics and culture, where the term is broadly used to cover the growing connections between societies worldwide. At one level it seems as if we live in a world where globalization has become part of everyday life. In almost any major world city you can see the familiar yellow M signalling the presence of a McDonald's fast food outlet. Globalization can be seen as focusing on the marketplace and the availability of goods around the world. Brands such as McDonald's have global status because of their market availability. This is an availability that is the result of the successful promotion of US products across the globe. This has extended to parts of the world that it was previously thought the US market could not reach, for example Russia, China, the states of what was formerly Eastern Europe. This is a success measured by the presence of a McDonald's in Beijing and Budapest and even the advertisement shown on US television in 1997 of the Russian President Gorbachev in a Pizza Hut restaurant. Terms such as 'McDonaldification' and Disneyfication' have been coined to describe, albeit somewhat simplistically, this marketing phenomenon. The whole process has become much more sophisticated, as Naomi Klein argues, taking a critical stance on global marketing, in her book *No Logo* (2001). Klein argues that it is no longer possible to identify the signs of US-dominated marketing and we are presented with a cultural mix, what she calls a 'market masala'. This 'masala' involves a cultural mix, for example in advertisements targeted at young people in the 'teen market' of black and white 'Rasta braids, pink hair, henna hand painting, piercing and tattoos, a few national flags . . . Cantonese and Arabic lettering and a sprinkling of English words' (2001: 120). Klein claims that this kaleidoscope represents a new departure in globalized markets.

> Today the buzzword in global marketing isn't selling America to the world, but bringing a kind of market masala to everyone in the world . . . a bilingual mix of North and South, some Latin, some R&B, all couched in global party

lyrics. This ethnic-food-court approach creates a One World placelessness, a global mall in which corporations are able to sell a single product in numerous countries without triggering the old cries of 'Coca-Colonization' . . . By embodying corporate identities that are radically individualistic and perpetually new, the brands attempt to inoculate themselves against accusations that they are in fact selling sameness.

(Klein 2001: 117–18)

There is evidence of shared, globally comprehensible culture, through television – especially MTV, broadcast in eighty-three countries in the late 1990s (ibid.: 120) – films, the news media and the Internet. There is not only the food and drink that originate in the United States, like McDonald's and Coca-Cola, but a hybrid gastronomical culture which mixes a wide range of local cultures. For example in any UK city one can see a huge range of different restaurants representing myriad different cultures and the mingling of different traditions. For example the fish and chip shop is very likely to sell pizza, spring rolls and donner kebab as well as the traditional cod or haddock and chips. 'Texmex' food, another amalgamated cross-cultural hybrid, is widely available in supermarkets. Postcolonial cooking involves the mixing of different cultures and traditions across the globe and sometimes unusual, new combinations. The Balti cooking that people consume in what may be called 'Indian restaurants' in the UK, derived from a UK city, Birmingham, and not the Indian subcontinent. Not only is there a plethora of restaurants catering for different cultural tastes and traditions, but supermarkets stock goods from all over the world and the ingredients to prepare dishes that originate from diverse cultures.

This diversity extends to a whole range of cultural and artistic practices and experiences. Popular music draws upon an extensive and very mixed repertoire of traditions to produce new manifestations of fusion music and world music, although there is also a dominance of techno rhythms that masquerade as innovatory and diverse. The most exciting of contemporary art forms draw upon traditions and techniques that cross continents, times and experiences. There has been an explosion of communication technologies such as television and radio broadcasting and the Internet. The Internet provides very fast communication across the globe with an immediacy that has been hitherto unknown. Call centres receiving queries from people in the UK might be located in Glasgow or in Calcutta. Communication by electronic mail greatly facilitates the transmission of information about markets. Financial markets cover the globe and communicate and operate across national boundaries. In many cases the huge multinational companies not only dominate local markets but also their powers cross the borders of nation states.

Not only do US and other producers reach global markets and draw on the raw material from across the globe, the production process has been moved to occupy diverse global sites. For example many UK companies have shifted their production plants to 'lower cost' countries. Dr. Martens boots and shoes has moved from Northampton in England to China, where, instead of paying wages of £300 a week the company only need pay £20 a month (*The Guardian* 26 October 2002). Jensen has moved its car manufacture from Merseyside in the UK to South Africa and Royal Doulton, makers of traditional English china, has moved from Staffordshire to Indonesia (*The Guardian* 3 July 2002). These are all examples from 2002. They follow in the wake of many earlier moves. Of course movement goes both ways, with earlier examples of Japanese car production moving to the UK in the 1980s. A market slump or boom in one part of the world can send repercussions across the globe with which nations are unable to deal. Even within the west, a crisis on Wall Street or in a US-based multinational company, can mean pensions are at risk and endowment policies will fail to provide the monies required to pay off the mortgages on people's homes in the UK. (I have used the term the 'west' as a shorthand term of reference for the advanced, industrialized countries including North America, Europe and Australia and New Zealand, but I am aware that the word is deeply problematic. To use the 'west' may suggest an opposition to something which might be called the 'east', as Edward Said (1978) has pointed out. Thus one might appear to be asserting, not only the sameness of all countries involved in each category but the superiority in all respects of that which is called the 'west'. Some writers prefer to use Euro-American, which seems just as limited. My use of the 'west' is practical and avowedly limited but serves to provide a category for parts of the world that have particular economic and political histories.)

Global climate changes impact upon everyone, not least upon those in less-developed and less-affluent regions of the world, who have least resources with which to cope with the devastation of floods, drought or earthquakes, which might result from climate change. Many of these changes have been initiated by some of the excessive patterns of energy consumption in the west. Globalization in this context can be seen to have significantly negative effects upon people across the world.

Globalization is subject to considerable debate within the social sciences because of its impact upon our daily lives. As Anthony Giddens stresses in the introduction to his 1999 Reith lectures, many of the effects of globalization are positive. He claims that globalization:

> also influences everyday life as much as it does events happening on a world scale . . . in parts of the world women are staking claim to greater autonomy than in the past and are entering the labour force in large numbers. Such aspects of globalisation are at least as important as those happening in the global market-place. They contribute to the stresses and strains affecting traditional ways of life and cultures in most regions of the world . . . other traditions, such as those affecting religion, are also experiencing major transformations.
>
> (Giddens 2002: 4)

The debate within the social sciences is focused around the arguments about the extent of globalization. Is it really that new? The other important dimension of this debate is the tension between those who see globalization as largely beneficial and who see its transformative characteristics as far outweighing any of its disadvantages, on the one hand, and those who point to its most destructive, largely western-led dominance, on the other.

At some moments the impact of what can be called globalization is much more alarming than at others. The merging of cultures, for example in relation to food, dress and music and improved communication and transport systems may seem to offer exciting possibilities for new developments and new experiences. However, interconnections between societies can also illustrate the wide differences and inequalities that exist alongside the apparently more anodyne and even positive aspects of globalization. This can be demonstrated in one of the experiences of the twenty-first century that involved the meeting of very different worlds.

Summary

- Globalization involves connections between different countries, their economies and cultures across the world.
- It is a key term in the social sciences because of its impact upon our daily lives.
- This impact ranges from the relatively mundane everyday merging of different cultures to significant, often destructive events on the world scale.
- Globalization involves economic, social, political and cultural aspects of life.
- There are different views on the impact of globalization, as positive or negative, and even on the extent of its impact.

Different worlds

ACTIVITY

Look at Plate 6.1. What does it mean to you? What can the events recorded here tell us about globalization?

COMMENT

There are many different responses to the image presented here. It is shocking. In many parts of the world the image will be very familiar as it has been reproduced so many times, to signify the shock that this invasion of the US heartland provoked. The photographic image and the date of the event have themselves become symbolic of the US experience, so much so that the event is known by the US way of recording the date, 9/11, with the month preceding the day.

Plate 6.1 9/11: the World Trade Center
Courtesy: Jeff Christensen/Reuters/Popperfoto.

It is a scene of unthinkable destruction, in a world where we are familiar with such scenes of devastation, but in 'other' parts of the world; not in the United States and not in New York. On 11 September 2001, with the destruction of the twin towers of the World Trade Center in New York and of part of the Pentagon in Washington, the United States was plunged into a state of war against an enemy who could not be immediately identified. More alarming even than the devastation and destruction of life on US soil was the immediate uncertainty about who had committed the atrocity and thus the uncertainty about the action which should be taken. What was certain is that the United States, its way of life and what it embodied, had been attacked. It was a shocking reminder that everyone is vulnerable to acts of terrorism, even in the most powerful, most protected and most affluent of countries.

In some ways this image challenges the notion that we live in a globalized world. We live in a world marked by conflict and opposition, which is experienced even at the heart of one of the world's most affluent and most powerful nations. However, the attack did involve a significant crossing of borders of *nation states*. The occasion has achieved such iconic status because it involved such a hostile attack on US territory. Not since the Japanese bombing of Pearl Harbor, with which the events of 9/11 were compared, has the United States been so attacked. 9/11 was clearly about one world clashing with another, but not about the attack by one *nation* on another. At first the United States was very unsure about the identity of its enemy. No nation state had declared war upon the United States either formally or by the implications of its actions, as in the case of Pearl Harbor. This was made clear by the US president in his first address to the American people on 15 September 2001, when George W. Bush described the conflict in the following terms:

> This is a conflict without battlefields or beachheads, a conflict with opponents who believe they are invisible . . . Those who make war against the United States have chosen their own destruction . . . We are planning a broad and sustained campaign to secure our country and eradicate the evil of terrorism.
>
> (*The Observer* 16 September 2001: 3)

This was an enemy of the United States who seemed to be invisible because it was not an enemy associated with a particular state or even a group of states. In a sense this is very much a globalized enemy, one without a state, with no immediately recognizable base in any particular nation with a government against which the United States might retaliate. The enemy was identified as terrorism and what is called terrorism crosses the boundaries of the nation state. Al Qu'eda, the terrorist organization later seen as responsible for the attacks on the World Trade Center and the Pentagon, was characterized by its transnational networks. Transnational networks are a feature of such terrorist groups, which operate outside and across the boundaries of nations, employing a diverse range of networks, all of which are heavily dependent on new technologies and Internet communication, as well as drawing on traditional religious affiliations and loyalties. There is no simple opposition between the high-tech west and the low-tech 'outsiders', terrorists or guerrilla fighters. There are complex interconnections between these different worlds. The technologies, many of which might have been generated and financed in the west, especially in the United States, are utilized across national boundaries. The pilots who flew the planes involved on September 11 were trained in the west, even in the United States. The separation between the two worlds is complex. However, there are marked distinctions between the access to resources and overall levels of poverty and affluence in these different worlds. Giddens argues that the greatest dangers to the advanced industrial nations, like the United States, come not from other such nations but from

> failed or collapsing states, together with the fears and hatreds such situations engender . . . Countries struggling against poverty, bearing the long-term impact of colonialism and the Cold War, or both, and where government lacks legitimacy, are breeding grounds for resentment and despair. They can become havens for transnational networks, which as the rise of Al-Queda showed, can provide a very real source of threat to the integrity of nations.
>
> (Giddens 2002: xiv)

Globalization can be read as the ever-increasing dominance of western, in particular US, economic, political and cultural systems across the world. Such an attack as that of 11 September 2001 can also be seen as a response to aspects of globalization and the perceived threat to non-western traditions of religion, culture and politics. The desperation of terrorists can be seen in response to the ever-increasing influence of western economics and thought, especially of western secularization, and the need to assert their own values in a globalized world. Global stakes are high and however far-reaching the political, economic and cultural mix may seem to be global, the world is still characterized by oppositions, especially those based on inclusion and exclusion. The events of September 11 illustrate some of the underlying conflicts and inequalities in the experience of globalization. The key questions are: Whose culture, whose way of life is dominant? Who has power and who is threatened?

Summary

The example of 9/11 illustrates some aspects of globalization:

- Globalization may involve conflict as well as consensus in the inter-connections between countries that are taking place across the globe.
- Globalization is characterized by a crossing of the boundaries of nation states.

- New media technologies and communication systems play a crucial part in the processes of globalization.
- The transmission of visual images and reports of people's experience can be conveyed at speed and almost universally, thus giving particular meaning to certain events like 9/11.
- Globalization can be seen as bringing together very different worlds and as highlighting the inequality between them.
- Globalization may involve conflict and inequality as well as consensus and new opportunities.
- There are different views on the impact of globalization and on its outcomes, especially in relation to the inequalities that can result.

Globalization

The impact and extent of globalization is strongly contested, but it clearly has a part to play in the movement of peoples and the disruption that took place in the twentieth century. I have already suggested some of the main features of globalization: the crossing of national boundaries by financial concerns, political, social and cultural systems, the interconnection between states and the impact of new technologies. What else can we add to define globalization? Given that there is considerable disagreement, what areas of agreement might there be? Globalization involves:

- A complex process whereby connections between people in different places across the globe are becoming faster and more closely linked.
- Movement of people, goods and services and information across the globe, characterized by range, intensity and speed.
- An explosion of global trade with the development of new communications and deregulation of markets and, especially within OECD (Organization for Economic Co-operation and Development) states a vast expansion in exports, employment and technology investment, controlled by multinational corporations.
- The reduction of sovereignty of nation states, although there has been an increase in the formation of new nation states, for example following the break-up of the USSR.
- New relationships between the local and the global are being developed through new networks.
- Global migrations including flows of refugees and asylum seekers on a massive scale.
- Environmental crises on a larger scale than ever before experienced, and there is much greater perception of risk than in the past.

Globalization is frequently categorized by different dimensions, such as economic and political processes, social relations, the role of technologies or its environmental impact. Discussion of globalization has often focused on the growth of economic globalization and the demise of the importance of the nation state and of local cultures in the face of global culture, and on the role of new technologies in opening up possibilities for change. At the basis of this issue are questions about the all-encompassing forces of globalization. The scale and scope of the different phenomena associated with globalization suggest that there are imbalances of power and that there might be a much stronger weighting in favour of the agency and control of some parts of the world and on the part of some protagonists. Some debates have focused on the imbalance between the local and the global and there are conceptualizations of the local–global tension framed in the language of winners and losers (for further discussion see Held 2000). Held himself posits an alternative to the extremes of the globalizers who see globalization as imposing enormous economic and political changes, and the opposing, more traditionalist view that argues that far from being a massive, new phenomenon, globalization has a long history and recent changes have not completely undermined state powers. His view supports the notion that 'globalization is creating new economic, political and social circumstances which are serving to transform state powers and the context in which states operate . . . politics is no longer and can no longer be, simply based on nation-states' (2000: 3). This approach claims that the outcomes of globalization are neither fixed nor clear. It is a phenomenon that can be harnessed. Thus globalization offers opportunities for 'redefining the role and functions of national government, emphasizing its potential strategic co-ordinating role – the intelligent state or the competition state – as opposed to the interventionist, redistributive state of the post-war era . . . [and] stress investment in human capital and technical skills – to make national economies more competitive – as against the provision of "passive" welfare benefits' (Held and McGrew 2000: 250). In this sense Held's view is positioned between those of the positive and the negative globalists, in what he and his colleagues call the transformationalist view.

Positive globalists see a range of benefits for everyone in the processes that have been taking place. For example Thomas Friedman (1999) has argued that the era of globalization has been one of peace, because the economic links have led to greater overall prosperity, which has created strong interests for all in the development of those relationships. Such views even suggest that poorer countries benefit particularly from increasing efficiency of markets, which has been another outcome of globalization. The American Foreign Policy Association produced a study which concluded that, using the criteria of information technology, finance, trade, politics, travel and personal communication, the world's most globalized countries have achieved greater income equality than their less globalized counterparts (American Foreign Policy Association 2002).

This approach is countered by the more negative views of globalization, for example J. K. Galbraith (1999) has argued that the forces of competition, deregulation and privatization have been disastrous for the world's poorest people. This perspective is supported by feminist critiques, some of which are discussed in more detail below. For example Jill Steans has commented that 'the least unionized and poorest paid of all workers, women have been particularly vulnerable to the market policies which have continued to characterize global economic restructuring in the 1990s' (2000: 368).

There are optimistic and pessimistic approaches to globalization and some argue that its importance has been overestimated (Thompson 2000). Globalization and the technologies associated with it necessarily involve the crossing of national boundaries. This means that there is increasingly a transnational dimension to economic, social, political and cultural life. Anthony Giddens has stressed the plurality of globalization and its multidimensional processes. What he describes in his 1999 Reith lectures, as a 'Runaway World', involves both the erosion of traditional boundaries as well as the increasingly interdependent aspects of globalization (2002). He stresses the ways in which the world has become a single social system as a result of growing ties of interdependence with social, political and economic connections cross-cutting borders between countries and impacting on those living within them. Giddens acknowledges some of the inequities involved in these processes, but argues against the claim that globalization means Americanization and everyone becoming the same and for an optimistic approach, which stresses the creation of new opportunities and developments. He claims that processes involved in globalization open up opportunities more than they impose particularly dominant western–US cultural practices and systems.

Whilst globalization is clearly multifaceted, some facets have been given greater emphasis than others and those such as 'race' and gender, which are implicated in unequal relationships and contribute more to debates within development studies, have been subsumed or marginalized in the mainstream of globalization (Adam 2002). Saskia Sassen has argued that gender and race are key components in the global political economy. For example she shows how, in the global cities (1998), most of the daily servicing jobs in the financial sectors are carried out by women, immigrants and people from minority ethnic groups, often all three in the same person, since they are, of course, overlapping groups. This work is an integral part of globalizing processes, although they are not always recognized as such.

The rapid transmission of information across the globe and the spread of corporations, economic systems and cultures across national boundaries open up new networks and opportunities, as well as new means of expansion, dominance and exploitation. Time and space merge through the use of the Internet and even the telephone, where call centres dealing with customers' queries about their accounts may be based thousands of miles from the customers who call them. In this sense space and time are shrinking. Information technologies facilitate very rapid communications across the globe and people can be physically transported in journeys that cover extensive distances in a very short time. Cultural products, films, music and television programmes are transmitted across the globe so that they are no longer the cultural property of one place. The key question now is not so much what period in chronological time do we find ourselves, nor in what geographical space, but in what time–space (Bauman and May 2001). The elision of time and space is a transforming feature of globalization. However, the compression of time and space may, at times, be overemphasized to underplay material and economic inequalities that are still experienced by many people across the globe. Time in this relationship is the speed of communication, not human experience of daily life. Images and information may be transmitted very fast, but this does not necessarily alter people's experience of birth, life and death nor the experience of poverty through that life course.

Manuel Castells (1997) has argued that the concept of the *network* is crucial to the global process of interconnection, for example through communications networks such as those of information technologies. He suggests that the speed and efficiency of contemporary global communications networks create new power relationships. Networks provide a new material basis that can shape social structures themselves. According to Castells (1996), the power of globally networked financial flows takes precedence over the flows of power. The 9/11 example illustrates some of the more sinister operations that are possible for global networks. Al Qu'eda is a global network combining human resources, most likely men, machines, technology, training and other financial networks deployed to finance terrorist activities. Terrorist movements like Al Qu'eda are a network that appears to have no boundaries, no specific beginning (or end). Castells is writing about a wider range of networks, however. These are networks that involve money, the global media, the Internet and social movements, travelling people as well as terrorist organizations. These include the global networks of corporations like McDonald's, which cross space and time, overcoming regional and national boundaries, through the production and consumption of their products (all of which are the same). There is some fluidity in the operations of such networks in that they cross the boundaries of nation states and the specific cultures associated with particular regions, although the products so promoted may show a striking uniformity. Network theories may also overemphasize the universal processes that are involved. There are significant differences between the experiences of different people. There are regional, cultural and ethnic differences, all of which illustrate some of the inequities that are involved in the operation of global networks.

One significant area of difference, which is often overlooked by network theorists, is that of gender. For example women's experience of the networked society in developing countries is not the same as men's. If women are employed at all by transnational corporations, they are likely to be employed in the most vulnerable posts and at the lowest levels of remuneration. Also, as Barbara Adam argues, for women in developing countries, 'when the torrent of networked financial flows rushes past you in a parallel universe, you may be thrown off balance by the accompanying waves, but for the rest of your life the established flows of power continue to reign supreme' (2002: 8). The point is not only that globalization involves uneven development and inequality, but that inequalities are experienced differently by different people and much of the globalization literature has omitted one of the most strongly experienced areas of difference, namely gender (Visvanathan *et al.* 1997).

Not everyone has equal access to the most powerful new technologies, although there may be some cultural democracy in the availability of new products and entertainment worldwide. Men's football offers a good illustration of some of the processes involved in the globalization of culture. Football is included under the umbrella term of culture! *Culture* is a term that has a variety of meanings and applications, including the distinction between 'high' and 'low' culture. This distinction was somewhat value laden, with those activities, practices and representational systems classified as 'high' culture being more highly valued than those classed as 'low'. This was the sort of distinction that might have claimed that opera was 'high' culture and football was 'low'. This was a dichotomy that was challenged by the 'cultural turn' in the social sciences (Hall 1997). My use here involves more of the anthropological understanding of culture, which includes all that characterizes the way of life of a group of people, whether this is a community, a nation or any other social group. Anthropology is concerned with finding out about how particular groups of people make sense of their lives and the symbols and practices that they deploy that may be distinctive to them and characteristic of their way of life. Culture includes all the ways we have of making sense and of making meanings. This understanding of culture might also appear to stress shared meanings and the ways in which people who share a culture might have a common set of understandings about the world, or more specifically the community, they live in.

Summary

- Different approaches to globalization can hold positive or negative views or present a middle, transformationalist course.
- An emphasis on 'winners' sees everyone benefiting from expansion.
- Losers miss out on the benefits and are further exploited by globalization.
- Global networks and flows operate differently for different groups of people.

Cultural globalization: a sporting diversion

Men's football presents a useful case study of globalized culture that might appear to offer a positive view of the accessibility of global culture. Football might seem to be a very popular activity in which people across the world can participate, especially as spectators of the game and as fans of the big clubs. Indeed, so popular is men's football that it can be seen as recruiting more followers than any other activity or even belief (Goldblatt 2002). The game is truly cosmopolitan as illustrated by the World Cup with the financial investment, politics and passion it evokes. However, it is at club level that the deepest passions might be implicated especially involving the mass of popular support. Football makes money for elites and for its top celebrity players, but it is also an enormously popular sport among ordinary people, women and men, in the communities in which they live. However, club football also goes global, and not only by participating in international competitions. Manchester United is the richest and the most well-known club in the UK and most likely in the world. It has the largest worldwide following, with more fans in China than in Manchester, or indeed in the UK. Fans around the world wear the Manchester United strip to signify their interest in football. At some moments it might appear that Manchester United is synonymous with the game. For example spectators at the African Nations Cup can be seen wearing different Manchester United home and away strip, even though the club does not play in this competition, nor have any members of the club been in this all-African tournament.

It may be possible for almost anyone around the world, provided they have the resources, to watch Manchester United on satellite television and indeed to identify themselves as supporters of the club, and to purchase versions of the club strip. However, there are wide discrepancies between those who view and those who decide what is to be seen, and those who buy into the culture and those who make profits from communications networks (Plate 6.2).

So powerful are these networks that it is probably unlikely that anyone reading this will have no idea what Manchester United football team and the whole commercial synergy that accompanies it, are. Men's football offers a particularly good example of the globalization of culture, economics and politics, with the development of the men's game growing out of the relative autonomy of nation states' regulation and control of their own football associations. More countries belong to FIFA, the world football organizing body, than to any other international body. The English game, in spite of the relative lack of success by the national

Plate 6.2 Global marketing? Manchester United Megastore
Source: © EMPICS Sports Photography.

Plate 6.3 Global fandom
Source: © EMPICS Sports Photography.

team, which is still living nostalgically off the glory of the 1966 World Cup victory, still plays a significant global role especially through the dominance of particular clubs, like Manchester United, with their associated cultural synergies. In the 2002 men's World Cup, Manchester United as a team, and its star players, who also played for the England side, had a huge following in Japan and South Korea, even though this was an international competition and not one involving clubs (Plate 6.3). Certain clubs, like Manchester United, supersede the national team.

Men's football has huge capital investment and, until very recently, up to the crisis of ITV Digital, was cash rich from satellite television with enormous global media coverage, which has built on and massively extended grass roots support. Recent crises are unlikely to have much negative impact on the really big clubs though. By 1998, men's football's global appeal was indicated by the entry of 173 nations in the World Cup that year (Armstrong and Giulianotti 1999) and just over 200 in 2002 (Goldblatt 2002). The 'World Cup' means the men's competition. It is only the Women's World Cup that is gendered in the naming, another indication of the ways in which globalization can appear to be gender neutral and conceal the very different and unequal experiences of women and men in the processes involved. Women's football suffers from the dominance of men's football and its occupation of the mass cultural media stage.

Summary

- Football is a global sport with massive participation which makes it truly a globalized cultural activity, involving a range of technologies and media.
- Economic dimensions of globalization include financial investment, the enormous profits generated by the game, the huge transfer charges for celebrity players, the synergy of products associated with the game, especially the big clubs.
- Political aspects indicate the crossing of national boundaries; the big clubs all have a large number of players of different nationalities and a governing body that crosses the boundaries of individual nation states.
- Football is a mass involvement phenomenon.
- Football, like other global activities and cultures, involves inequalities and exclusions, for example related to gender.
- There are winners and losers, for example the big clubs and those in lower leagues who cannot finance buying in new players.

Movement of people: migration

Not only does globalization facilitate the transmission of culture across the globe, it is also characterized by the movement of peoples, another key feature of globalization. Migration is not, of course, a new phenomenon but it has become an important part of the notion of movement of ideas, resources and people which go to make up globalization. Why do people migrate? The movement of peoples and itinerant communities were features of ancient societies. There is some overstatement in the claim that migration is a recent phenomenon. Migration not only has a long history, it has different dimensions. Incentives to migrate often take the form of economic forces. People move across the globe in order to do paid work, either because they have no such work where they currently live or because they want to improve their circumstances and seek opportunities elsewhere. People have long moved to facilitate access to food and resources. Increasingly the motivation to migrate is tied up with economic factors. It can be argued that in the modern period, from the fifteenth century, migration has been closely linked to labour power. The movement of people has been tied to economic factors on a large scale, whether that movement has been the result of coercion or has been the outcome of voluntarily made decisions – that is the result of 'push' or 'pull' factors. As Saskia Sassen has argued, there are reasons why people migrate. Migrations 'do not "just happen": they are one outcome . . . in a more general dynamic of change' (1998: 116). Much of the recent discussion of globalization has centred on the extent of migration across the globe and the developments that have facilitated the speed and frequency of global movements of people. Migrations have taken place across large areas and have involved both the compulsion of 'push' factors, including threats of violence and of starvation, and the draw of 'pull' factors, with economic, social and political incentives. Contemporary debates and media coverage – especially, as was illustrated in Chapter 3, about refugees seeking asylum in European countries – also oversimplify the categories and the motivating factors behind migration, by separating out economic migrants from those who are classified as political refugees. 'Political' refugees, classified as deserving refuge, are set apart from economic migrants, who are deemed to be seeking advancement and not deserving of refuge, in a binary logic that underplays the complexity of the operation of 'push' and 'pull' factors and the distinctions between the political and the economic. Political and cultural factors may deny participation in economic life and this can operate in more or less traumatic ways. It has been dramatic, as in the case of the expulsion of East African Asian people from Uganda by Idi Amin, and has been accompanied by violent action as in Afghanistan, the former Yugoslavia and, with catastrophic consequences, in Rwanda, but the interplay of different forces is not always so dramatically and publicly enacted. The interpretation of migration as motivated by either push or pull factors can underplay the different experiences among migratory peoples and overemphasize the homogeneity of any group of people who are leaving their homes to settle in another place.

The German writer Bertolt Brecht described his own experience of exile from Nazi Germany during the years 1933–48, in his poem *Concerning the Label Emigrant*

> I always found the name false which they gave us: Emigrants.
> That means those who leave their country. But we
> Did not leave, of our own free will
> Choosing another land
> . . .
> Merely, we fled. We are driven out banned.
> Not a home but an exile, shall the land be that took us in.
>
> (in Jarvis 2002: 80)

Migration across the globe can have negative or positive outcomes and sometimes both. Refugees are sometimes able to escape the horror of oppressive regimes in their own country and gain sanctuary in the place to which they migrate. People do achieve considerable success in their new home, but they can also meet with hostility and resentment, which might go a long way towards offsetting the relief they feel.

Lydia Potts (1990) argues that some contemporary discussion of migration, in the context of globalization, fails to explore the power imbalances and inequities that are involved, especially those relating to race and gender. A focus on the exploitative dimensions of migration in relation to labour, yields very different understandings of the opportunities for those who migrate from more optimistic readings. Potts argues that human beings as 'living labour power' have been transferred in large quantities and over long distances since the end of the fifteenth century. This period covers the enslavement of the Indians that followed the conquest of America, various forms of forced labour and forced migration in Latin America, Asia and Africa, African slavery and the coolie system used to despatch the people of Asia all over the world. In the present day there is labour migration, the search for political asylum and the brain drain, including the exodus of academics from developing countries to the west. Potts stresses the lack of freedom for the people who were involved in these migrations. In the past, as now, the global market for labour often involves exploitation especially along the lines of gender and race.

Migration is experienced differently by women and by men and by people of different ethnic backgrounds. At many historical points it has been men who have played the major role in migration. In enforced migration, this has taken the form of the enslavement of larger numbers of men than women or, more recently, men have left their homes to look for work before women. Migrant workers are however often assumed to be male and little attention is given to the specific circumstances of women. Migration has different meanings at particular times in history and for different groups of people. Potts's argument points to the need to question first, the idea that migration as part of globalization is a new phenomenon and second, to challenge the argument that migration is always from choice and is a liberatory experience for those involved.

Summary

- Migration is an important aspect of globalization.
- Migration is not new but can be seen as having intensified over the last century.
- Migration involves complex factors, political, social, economic and cultural, which it is difficult to separate; they interrelate.
- Different people have different experiences of migration, for example women and men and people of different ethnicities.

Equality, inequality, risk and danger

The events of 9/11 may have provided an important illustration of the vulnerability of all those who inhabit this planet, including the most powerful. Terrorist attacks are certainly not confined to the powerless in their target, although it may well be the lack of power and lack of resources which prompts the participation in terrorist activities. As Saskia Sassen (2001) argued after 9/11, the rich countries discovered that they could not insulate themselves from the poor and destitute and hide behind their prosperity. Terrorism strikes at the most affluent heart of western states. Sassen claims that the debt and growing poverty of what she calls the south, that is the developing world and those countries outside the wealthy west, are connected to terrorist acts such as 9/11. The growth of poverty and debt have led to large-scale migration into the ever more wealthy, and hence ever more attractive, countries of the west. Sassen describes terrorism as a 'language of last resort', through which those on the outside endeavour to make themselves heard in the rich countries of the world.

It is frequently the less powerful and the poorest societies that are the victims, notably of environmental degradation and disaster, which are also features of the globalized economy. Environmental danger and risk is not entirely selective in its impact. There may also be some human agency involved in the location of environmental dangers and disasters. In her 2000 Reith lecture on poverty and globalization, Vandana Shiva argued against complacency about the benefits of globalization. She claimed that many of the 'natural disasters' experienced in the developing world are not natural at all, but 'man-made'. She cites the example of a drought which is 'the result of mining scarce ground water in arid regions to grow thirsty cash crops for exports instead of water prudent food crops for local needs' (2000: 1). Similarly, the ecological and social disaster of the Punjab, formerly one of the most productive and prosperous agricultural areas in India, she attributes to heavy use of pesticides, which have killed the pollinators. Vandana Shiva makes a strong case against a positive view of economic globalization.

> It is women and small farmers working with biodiversity who are the primary food providers in the Third World, and contrary to the dominant assumption, their biodiversity based on small farms are more productive than the industrial monocultures.
>
> The rich diversity and sustainable systems of food production are being destroyed in the name of increasing food production . . . Planting only one crop in the entire field as a monoculture will of course increase its individual yield. Planting multiple crops in a mixture will have low yields of individual crops, but will have a high total output of food.
>
> (Shiva 2000: 2)

Here Shiva's point is about politics as well as agricultural practice and it is impossible to disentangle the two. The political power relations to which she refers involve the tensions between the different worlds of the affluent west and global capital on the one hand and of the developing, largely poor world on the other, as well as the particular exploitation of women in the developing world. 'And women themselves are devalued. Because many women in the rural and indigenous communities work co-operatively with nature's processes, their work is often contradictory to the dominant market driven "development" and trade policies'(ibid.: 3). The global inequalities involved in the inequitable experience of environmental degradation and danger have been highlighted by the anti-globalization movement. This movement has drawn attention to the unequal balance of power and inequitable distribution of resources across the globe. This imbalance not only leads to the overuse of resources by the developed, largely western world, but also the environmental degradation arising from that exploitation and overuse of resources.

The inequality between the powerful and the powerless was well illustrated in the World Summit on Sustainable Development in Johannesburg in 2002. The summit was attended by delegates from 190 nations, with per capita incomes in US $ ranging from Ethiopia with 101 and Burundi with128, to France and the UK with 24,287 and 24,323 respectively. The president of the world's richest nation, the United States, with a per capita income of $32,778 (UN data 1999, in *The Guardian* 10 September 2002) did not attend. At this Earth Summit there was a stark contrast between those with power, land and resources and those without, represented by a particularly strong visual image which was shown on news coverage: the landless protestors occupied an area in the Soweto township a very short distance from the conference centre, the entrance to which was dominated by a stand promoting the expensive German-made car, BMW. The contrast between those who have no land and in a rural economy no means of securing a livelihood, with a product, which consumes resources beyond the strictly necessary, and creates environmentally damaging carbon monoxide, is stark. Of course, the situation is much more complex than this opposition suggests. One emphasis of the 2002 summit was on collaboration with major companies but it is a graphic example of inequality. However, opinions differed greatly about how much had been achieved at this summit and the unwillingness of the United States to commit itself to any environmental policies was instrumental in the failure to agree on more meaningful targets, for example on trade, globalization and poverty. Substantial progress was made on the issue of water and sanitation with an agreed commitment to halving the number of people without basic sanitation to 1.2 billion by 2015 and to provide clean water for half of those without it. However, these targets are not legally binding and do not incur sanctions if they are not met. Any progress on water and sanitation might be somewhat offset by the failure of the United States and Australia to agree to the Kyoto protocol on the reduction of carbon dioxide emissions (*The Guardian* 10 September 2002: 68). Globalization, especially economic globalization can be seen as partly contributing to, and exacerbating such inequality. This inequality is the focus of many of the movements against globalization (Plate 6.4).

One of the ways in which the problems have been experienced across the globe as a result of climate changes and the impact of contemporary patterns of production and consumption, have been described as environmental *risks*. What do we mean by risk? Risk involves hazard and even danger. An environmental risk suggests that the planet itself is in some danger and that people might be at risk in relation to the environment in which they live. We are familiar with some of these risks. They include risks in relation to the food we eat. Think of the health scares around BSE (bovine spongiform encephalopathy) or 'mad cow' disease, foot-and-

Plate 6.4 Anti-globalization demonstrations, 2002
Courtesy: Andrea Comas/Reuters/Popperfoto.

mouth disease in cattle and sheep, listeria in cheese and salmonella in eggs. All these food scares raised questions about how food is produced, what necessary safety precautions should be taken and the responsibility of human beings who participate in the processes of production. Risks related to the production process which are identified and manifested as 'scares' demand political intervention and it is difficult to disentangle the economic from the political factors. Other scares involve apparently 'natural' disasters. These include poor quality air and increases in respiratory diseases such as asthma arising from fossil fuel burning pollution, increased incidence of skin cancer and links with depletion of the ozone layer, along with floods and other 'natural' disasters affecting human health and well-being.

All such environmental hazards involve some human intervention or agency and are not simply 'natural'. They may be the result of human activity, such as feeding herbivorous animals such as cows with meat, including offal from diseased sheep. These human actions may be motivated by the need to increase *productivity*, to reduce production costs, to make ends meet or to increase profits. On the other hand, human intervention may take the form of defining what constitutes the 'risk'. Sociologists such as Ulrich Beck and Anthony Giddens argued that we live in the 'risk society' where the perception of risk is great and people feel they should take responsibility for dealing with these perceived risks (Beck 1992; Giddens 2002). It is suggested that technology in contemporary society is increasingly seen to be producing physical harm and the effect of such damage is not restricted by national boundaries. Such harm requires global management of risk (Giddens 2002). For example disasters such as Chernobyl have had global consequences, with impact as far afield as the UK where it is claimed sheep cannot be eaten in the north-west of England because of contamination by caesium 137 (Stacey 2000: 133). Beck (1992) suggests that science is no longer seen as protecting people from risks but as creating them. Environmental problems are linked to health problems. For example the depletion of the ozone layer with the increased danger of skin cancer. The idea that we could take some action to protect ourselves as individuals from these hazards creates a climate of fear and anxiety. This is exacerbated by the knowledge that the scares and even disasters may be the result of human action and not simply 'acts of God' or naturally induced. However, individuals have limited powers in protecting themselves from policies which have permitted practices that have created these problems in the first place.

The notion of 'risk' might be seen to imply an element of choice that danger does not suggest. Risk might even include some element of excitement and of gambling on one's chances, which the more material 'danger' does not imply. Beck's choice of the term 'risk' has some significance because of its focus on both the perception of human agents and its element of chance. Risk may carry less weight than danger which suggests no way of people addressing the problems they face and of effecting any changes in outcome.

Other social and material aspects of the environmental risks and dangers that accompany globalization involve the unequal experience of these dangers. For example natural disasters such as floods or even earthquakes have very different outcomes if they are experienced in more affluent countries such as the United States, for instance an earthquake along the San Andreas fault in California compared with one in a less well-resourced country such as Turkey. This is most likely to be the result of a disaster which cannot be said to be induced by the actions of human beings in any way. However, this is not to say that the disaster is purely natural and that it has no social implications. Another relevant factor might be the choice of human beings to live in the particular, disaster-prone area, although this is most likely to be a very limited choice for the poor. Those who are well off and whose communities are well resourced are better able to protect themselves with adequately built and supported housing and work accommodation.

Other disasters impacting upon the environment are more directly the result of human activity, such as at the Chernobyl nuclear power station and the United Carbide plant in Bhopal, India which killed thousands and left many more permanently disabled. These are examples of accidents resulting from the failure of those responsible for developments in technology. However, as the anti-globalization movement and Green activists have pointed out 'normal' economic developments and activities in a globalized world also have disastrous outcomes. The unprecedented growth of industrialized market economies over the past two hundred years have led not only to higher consumption but also to the degradation of the natural environment.

Summary

- Globalization can be seen as highlighting inequalities between different areas of the world.
- Environmental degradation can accompany globalization and contribute to the perception of risk.
- Environmental degradation involves social and political factors, as well as natural matters and the natural and the social interrelate.
- Environmental degradation and even natural disasters impact more upon the poor than the rich.
- Not only does massive economic expansion lead to the side effects of environmental problems, but the poor are less able to protect themselves than the well off.

Different views: weighing up the arguments

This discussion of some of the different aspects of the phenomenon of globalization illustrates some of the main tensions between social science approaches. One key aspect of the tension between different approaches relates to the definition of globalization, especially between those who see the phenomenon as a particularly important feature of the twentieth century, unprecedented in earlier times and being distinguished by the developments of new technologies of communication and those who do not. These different views on the phenomenon of globalization can be summarized by dividing the opposing approaches of those who argue that globalization is a significant new phenomenon into the category of globalizers and those who claim that globalization is not so new nor so important in explaining the experience of the twentieth and twenty-first centuries as non-globalizers (see Table 6.1).

Those who argue that globalization has been a most significant phenomenon which has unalterably changed social, cultural, political and economic life can be further subdivided into those who regard the changes effected through globalization as largely positive and who welcome the processes and those who take a more negative, pessimistic view, as summarized in Table 6.2.

Table 6.2 highlights the areas of difference in order to facilitate understanding of different views and also to provide a means of questioning a theoretical position. As was suggested in Chapter 3, there are different ways of evaluating and assessing the positions taken by social scientists is order to establish the strengths and weaknesses of their arguments; it was also suggested that one useful strategy was

Table 6.1 Features of globalizers and non-globalizers

	Globalizers	Non-globalizers
Definition of globalization	A real change in social processes A unified global culture and economy Very limited state sovereignty and autonomy	Globalization is not new Most economic and cultural activity is local/regional Traditional inequalities persist
Significance of contemporary globalization	Very important and wide reaching	No really important changes Globalizers too concerned with new technologies rather than material divisions
Impact of globalization	New global structures in politics, economics and cultural life Dominant financial and political institutions worldwide over and above national structures and institutions Large-scale migration of people	Nation states retain sovereignty and can determine own systems Cultural and social diversity remains Migration not in any way a new phenomenon

Table 6.2 Globalization: optimistic and pessimistic views

Optimistic views	Pessimistic views
Opportunities of Internet and greater democracy through online participation	Internet dominated by wealthy areas of world. Ignores differences of gender, race and material inequalities
Fast transmission of information	Speed of more importance to affluent nations
Easy access for individuals and community activists	Terrorist organizations benefit more than local communities
New opportunities for development of ideas and markets	Developing world not permitted to benefit. Environmental risk and degradation harsher in developing world
Access to cultural products for all across globe	Media dominated by US and western corporations
More choice	Choice only between western products
Easier movement of people across globe	Migration blocked for many refugees and migrants. Different experiences of exploitation by women
No state control of virtual space	

to pose the questions: *What is the evidence for this claim?* and *Does the claim cover everything? What are the gaps?* and *Does this claim make sense? Does the conclusion follow from the initial claims?*

Looking at alternative theoretical positions provides a useful entry into asking these questions. What is left out may be what is the focus of the alternative approach. For example the more positive claims that are made about globalization can be seen to omit the experience of the developing world and the inequalities created by the phenomenon. Asking the question 'who is left out' may well be presented to challenge claims that there can be the same experience for a group of people or even a society, which is necessarily diverse in terms of gender, ethnicity, age and disability. The more positive globalizers may omit the experiences of those who are on the margins of the benefits of globalization or who have specific experiences because of their gender or ethnicity. As has been argued above, women's and men's experiences of globalization are different.

Of course there are not only two perspectives on globalization. The two columns in Table 6.2 only represent one reading of possible oppositions in thinking about globalization. As was suggested above in the section on 'Globalization', there are approaches to the phenomenon that argue for its importance as part of the experience of living in the twenty-first century, but that its impact is both positive and negative. As propounded in the work of both Giddens and Held, globalization is seen to be transforming contemporary societies in all respects – political, economic, social – but has different impacts at different times and in different places. The theoretical approach to globalization adopted by social and political theorists such as Held and Giddens can be classified as transformationalist, because of their emphasis on significant, transforming changes. However, this approach challenges the dominance of a particular economy and culture and suggests that globalization does not make everyone the same; there is scope for resistance and for more local agency. This approach rejects the polarity of a globalizer versus non-globalizer division and supports more complex readings of the phenomenon, which permit some space for the independence of nation states on the world scene (Giddens 2002; Held *et al.* 1999).

Conclusion

This chapter has introduced the idea of globalization and has explored some of the ways in which it is defined and discussed within the social sciences, as well as the impact of some of the processes involved upon our daily lives. Globalization is an important concept in contemporary social science and, although the phenomenon has a long history, its most recent ramifications through the twentieth and into the twenty-first centuries can be seen as transforming human societies across the globe. This has been illustrated by examples of marketing and the production and consumption of a whole range of goods and services worldwide, as well as by the cultural diversity that is manifest in many areas of contemporary life. The more negative dimensions of globalization have been demonstrated by the impact of environmental degradation and political conflict, which, in trans-gressing boundaries between states, make everyone vulnerable. Acts of terrorism and terrorist networks have an impact on all people, including people in the most affluent and powerful nations.

Globalization is marked by inequality as well as by increased opportunities. This is what most concerns the social science explanations of the phenomenon. New technologies provide the possibility of optimistic readings based on greater democracy and opportunities for greater participation in political, social and economic life for all as well as speed and efficiency. However, there is still the danger of exclusion and of domination by the most powerful corporations and institutions at the expense of local communities. Optimistic readings of globalization often underplay the differences of ethnicity and gender which are crucial to the experience of globalization.

Chapter 7

Conclusion

How far have we come?

We have charted some of the big issues that are the subject of contemporary debate and identified some of the ways in which these issues have been addressed within the social sciences. Most of these 'big issues' are associated with change and transformation. For example we have considered the role of *identity* in a world that has fast-changing modes of communication and representation and a rapidly changing political landscape. Identity is a key concept for the exploration and understanding of the links between the personal and the social, that which connects the individual to the wider society. This has particular resonance in a world that appears to have become more uncertain as a result of economic, social, technological and political changes and developments, and has seen an increasing interest in the self in western societies. A focus on identity provides a means of assessing the impact of change and the ways in which people attempt to secure their identities in the midst of both continuities and transformations. The discussion of multiple identities draws in many of the other dimensions of social relations and organization, all of which are implicated in the relationship between the individual and the society.

The question of *citizenship* raises debates about changing social relationships and identities and the ways in which some groups of people have challenged their exclusion from the mainstream of social, economic and political life as represented by a full participation in citizenship. Citizenship offers another means of interrogating the extent of change and the forms it takes. As a re-formed category the notion of citizenship permits a fuller discussion of what is involved in the exclusion and marginalization of some people and, to counter this, the key elements in the promotion of greater social inclusion.

Another key area of change is the transformation of the role of consumption and of the relationship between *production* and *consumption*. The notion that we live in a 'consumer society' lends the term some status and centrality in contemporary debates. The extent of this change of emphasis has been both endorsed and challenged and the apparent shift towards patterns of consumption as assuming particular importance in contemporary societies has been the subject of some controversy. This focus on consumption raises questions about the need to explore other aspects of the process and the tension between earlier views, which attributed the greatest significance to production in shaping experience and social relations and divisions and more recent postmodernist approaches, with their focus on culture and representation.

An intensification of migration and the movement of peoples and a greater awareness of difference and diversity have led to a concern with the links between *place* and *race*. Current debates raise questions about the importance of place in shaping social relations. Place has been the focus of shifting explanations of social divisions, which have ranged from more local considerations of where people live to wider-scale consideration of the places we come from, the routes we have travelled and the places that have been important on those journeys. Place is linked to the construction of race and the experience of multiculturalism in contemporary societies. Race and ethnicity along with gender are aspects of difference that are central to current debates and thus to the issues addressed in this book.

Concern with place and movement, especially movement across the globe, whether of peoples, ideas, information or materials highlights another key area of current debate. The extent and impact of *globalization* has been of central concern both within the social sciences and in our everyday lives. We see daily reminders of economic and cultural globalization. The globalization of economic, social, political and cultural life presents issues that have to be addressed and assessed. However, there is considerable disagreement about the extent of globalization and about its impact, for example whether the phenomena associated with globalization have been beneficial or disadvantageous to different communities and different groups of people across the world. As I have argued, it is not an even process but one characterized not only by different perspectives, but also by significant inequalities. It is experienced differently by people in different parts of the world, especially the more affluent west, on the one hand, and parts of the developing world, on the other. Globalization has different impact on women than men and upon people from different ethnic groups. These are the substantive big issues that have formed the focus of each of the chapters in the book, but there are other, equally important debates involving key concepts, which have been woven through the discussion. The approach taken in this book has involved focusing on an interrogation of these issues, which has introduced some of the ways of thinking and, in particular, some of the important concepts in the social sciences.

Making sense of the issues; ideas that matter

Some key ideas have emerged through the discussion of the big issues in this book. You will have noticed that there are recurring themes and concepts. Some of these ideas are ones in common usage in everyday life, but they have particular meanings and applications within the social sciences.

Difference

The question of *difference* is one that has particular resonance. At several points we have considered what is meant by difference between and among people, and whether difference necessarily involves inequality, another key theme in this book. Difference is relational but as we have seen on many occasions it is also oppositional and involves the superiority of one group over another group which is identified as different, or 'other'; this is most marked in relation to race, ethnicity, gender and disability. Difference operates within the exchanges of everyday life and in the global arena, where it has been most marked in relation to global inequalities in some recent incidences of global terrorism and conflict. Difference also takes more positive forms in relation to cultural diversity and the opportunities afforded by new technologies and global transformation.

Inequality

Inequality has been deployed to draw attention to the ways in which the transformations of contemporary life often manifest traditional imbalances and inequities or create new forms, for example of exclusion. We have considered a range of examples of such imbalances that underpin many aspects of social relations, structures and institutions. Traditionally there has been an emphasis on social class as the main indicator of social divisions and inequality, but the study of social divisions has been extended to encompass many other dimensions of difference that are based on unequal power relations and an inequitable allocation of resources and civil rights. There have been a wide range of examples, such as gender, class, ethnicity and race, disability and the experience of migration. In many cases differences have been interpreted as involving an unequal relationship. For example, in the case of citizenship, the assumption of a white, male, able-bodied norm has involved the inequitable treatment of those who did not conform to this norm. Assumptions of homogeneity often conceal inequality. The impact of globalization has been uneven. The opportunities offered by new networks of communication, new technologies and economic globalization are not experienced equally across the globe, nor within specific communities and nations. Inequality has been another major issue in this book and has been linked to different manifestations of the unequal distribution of power.

Power

The issue of who can exercise *power* and who is denied access or has much more limited power raises questions about what we mean by power and most importantly how it is implicated in the structure of societies and the ways in which they are divided. As we have seen, this concept too is one which is both central to the social sciences and to addressing contemporary big issues, and strongly contested. We have looked at some of the developments in addressing the question of power in order to consider how it might be applied to current debates. Power can be seen as operating in a top-down relationship or as operating more diffusely in different situations. These discussions have taken us beyond the more common-sense assumptions that power must necessarily involve coercion and has led to some useful considerations of the ways in which power is produced, often in very indirect ways. There has been a shift from a discussion of the origins of power to an examination of how it operates, although the two are not necessarily mutually exclusive. It is possible to be eclectic, providing one supports the argument logically and with evidence. The purpose of the discussion in this book has been to show the importance of looking at how power operates and at its sources and how it is supported. There are examples of changes, not only in the conceptualization of the social sciences, but also in power relations both at a global level and in routine, everyday exchanges. Debates about how power operates are implicated in the experience of uncertainty in a changing world.

Change: uncertainty and diversity

Change creates uncertainty as well as new opportunities. The two necessarily interrelate at times of change. The speed and extent of change may create insecurities as well as radical, new possibilities. For example, technological change such as those related to reproductive technologies may create new opportunities for childless people to have their own babies, but along with these benefits go all the uncertainties about identity for those born through IVF, who may be unsure about who their genetic parents are. Societies may be enriched by the presence of a diverse range of peoples with different ethnic and cultural backgrounds and increased mobility may offer the chance to start a new life in different parts of the world. However, increased ethnic diversity may create insecurities that may lead to hostile reactions among other groups of people. The same social phenomena can lead to both positive and negative reactions by different groups of people. Uncertainty and diversity characterize social change, with different weightings in different situations at particular times.

Culture and meaning

The so-called 'cultural turn' has led to more of a concern with how meanings are produced and the mediation of culture in the understanding of social phenomena and relations. Many of the developments within the social sciences have turned to the need to explore the ways in which meanings are produced and have drawn attention to the crucial importance of representation and symbolic systems in shaping our perception of the world and our own place within it. For example we have looked at some of the ways in which race is a category that is represented and reproduced rather than reflecting any fixed truth or biological certainty. The meanings and values that are associated with the construction of race and with ethnicity are deeply embedded in cultural practices and histories. One of the ways of combating racism is to uncover some of these processes and to show how race is constructed and reproduced. Similarly, I have shown some of the ways in which economic processes such as the relationship between production and consumption are mediated by the culture, both through cultures of production and the production of culture. It is impossible to extricate consumption from the ways in which it is represented and the meanings that are associated with the goods and services which we consume. Throughout this book I have attempted to show that we have to unpack meanings and to show the associations that accompany symbolic systems, rather than implying that meanings are transparent and merely reflect the material world. The words, images, ideas and practices that form part of the cultural process are impossible to disentangle from the material world of which they make sense and which they represent.

Knowledge

Knowledge is both a key concept and a theme which has particular importance at this moment in history. In a 'knowledge society', the production and dissemination of knowledge has enormous significance. For example there has been massive intensification of the ways in which knowledge is produced and communicated at speed across the globe. We started with the example of education in Chapter 1, in order to highlight the importance of knowledge in the contemporary world. In our opening example access to education was presented as offering an escape from disadvantage and exclusion and an entry into a more privileged sphere where there are choices. Knowledge is an asset in the same way that finance and capital are assets. Knowledge is often the means of accessing higher rewards. In the 'information society' economic wealth increasingly flows to those who are more active in knowledge production and the communications revolution, especially those who are involved in the production, processing and control of knowledge. Traditional sources of authority have been challenged. In some cases there has been a democratization of knowledge with more people being able to access information and to make decisions about their own lives on the basis of that information. Sources of knowledge have changed, especially in terms of who has authority and who is classed as 'expert'. What is the role of the social sciences in this knowledge revolution? How are the social sciences implicated in the 'knowledge society'?

How do the social sciences address the big issues?

Most of the discussion in this book has involved identifying some of the big issues of contemporary concern and introducing some of the ways in which the social sciences address these issues. We have also considered the ways in which these big issues in the world are also central to debates within the social sciences. These debates begin with *questions*, notably questions about what is happening and how we can better understand the transformations that are taking place. The social sciences have specialist language just like other academic fields and one of the necessary processes involved in doing social science research is the development of new concepts to deal with the issues and problems that have been identified. Material and cultural transformations require specific ways of thinking and appropriate concepts to make sense of them. *Concepts* provide some of the organizing frameworks employed in order to make sense of what is happening in the contemporary world and, in particular in this book, of the changes that are taking place. Concepts have to relate to the world we live in in the ways in which it is organized and one of the means of exploring the usefulness of concepts is to examine the *evidence*. We have looked at many different sorts of evidence in this book, although there has not been any extensive discussion of the methods adopted by social scientists. The sources of evidence upon which social scientists draw range from quantitative material, for example relying on observational research methods and those which produce statistical data to more interpretative, qualitative evidence, such as interview material, first-person accounts and evidence that permits more of a voice to the people who are being studied. Some of the material we have looked at has been largely quantitative, such as the statistical data from *Social Trends*. Other sources have included media coverage of issues, such as newspaper articles and first-person accounts and interview material, such as those recorded in the Parekh Report, which would be categorized as more qualitative material. There is other material which can be included, such as fictional accounts, even poetry, all of which can give meaning to social issues.

Having reviewed the evidence there are *claims* that can be made, for example about how we might understand social phenomena. The claims that may be made on the basis of the evidence we have, have to be translated into an integrated explanatory *theory*, drawing on the evidence that has been cited in support of the claims made and developed in relation to other theoretical positions. The work of the social sciences is dynamic and constantly developing, both in relation to the evidence that is produced and the theoretical arguments that are re-negotiated and expanded. As I have suggested, one of the most important skills within the social sciences is the evaluation of different theories and the ways in which we can point to the weaknesses and omissions of one position in order further to support another perspective. There is an ongoing relationship between theories and evidence and the development of different theoretical approaches. This is what makes the social sciences exciting!

The social sciences

This book has covered the social sciences as if they constituted a shared body of concerns. Study in this area does illustrate shared characteristics across the different disciplines that make up the grouping that can loosely be called 'the social sciences'. However, each of the constituent disciplines has its own distinctive features as well as shared concerns in terms of areas of interest and methodologies. There has been a trend towards what has been called interdisciplinarity within the social sciences. For example each of the different disciplines that makes up the social sciences has addressed some of the key concepts that have been identified in this book and has approached a 'big issue' of contemporary concern, but employing some of the methods and theoretical approaches that are specific to that discipline. For example globalization has been of interest to all disciplines within the social sciences and, although they have taken different approaches, this can be seen as an indicator of an interdisciplinary position, where the phenomenon under investigation takes priority, rather than the traditional concerns of the discipline. However some disciplines have a different focus and you may feel that some of these areas might be of more interest to you than others.

While you have been reading this book you may well have found that you wanted to know more about the psychological issues that were raised by the material. In Chapter 2, some of the most important aspects of social identity are discussed. How do the social influences on identity get experienced at a psychological level? The discipline of psychology engages with questions about the relationship between the personal and the social, with a focus on the internal processes that are taking place. The discipline covers a wide range of issues and specific methods which are adopted to explore some of the investments that are made by individuals and by groups.

One of the themes of this book is the way in which society and nature combine. Psychology is a discipline that spans these two topics. At one end of the span, it looks at how society influences and is influenced by individuals. At the other end, it looks at how biology, for example the structure of the brain, influences and is influenced by individual behaviour and experience. Psychology covers a broad range, from language and social relationships to neurons and hormones. Social Psychology takes up many of the issues addressed in this book but with an emphasis on the experiences of people living within society. Whilst reading this book you have met various questions and topics that are closely related to the study of economics. We have looked at issues of work, consumption and inequality, and the relationship between production and consumption. The phenomenon of economic globalization has had a profound impact on people throughout the world. These are all essentially matters of concern to economists and involve both the interrogation of empirical data and theoretical dispute, for example between different approaches to globalization.

Economics requires an ability to handle its concepts, use of quantitative data and techniques and an interest in its methodological approaches, some of which focus on evidence which is presented in quantitative forms, such as statistical data. Economic issues also involve the workings of economies, for example particular economies in particular areas in the context of wider historical, political and cultural questions.

Many of the big issues picked out in this book have a political dimension, either directly or more widely. The discussions about gender, inequality, social class and nation are all relevant to political debates about social norms and political identities. Other arguments about citizenship and the environment directly relate to government policy making and wider social debate on these issues. You are also introduced to the key political idea of power and the discussion has included topics involved in central government policy-making areas. Different interpretations of the meaning of globalization illustrate a topic which governments around the world are having to manage. Many of the areas of change addressed in this book involve policy making, decision making and regulation at different levels ranging from communities to national governments and the global arena. As I have argued in this book, politics involves issues that impact upon our daily lives and may include personal and seemingly private issues related to sexuality and family as well the more obviously public arena of decision making and formal systems of policy making and legislation. Increasingly the study of politics considers politics and government in the context of broader cultural, social and economic trends.

Many of the big debates covered in this book are also those which are the subject of study in sociology. What is the relationship between individuals and the wider society? Are there more uncertainties in the contemporary world – about identity, about our perception of risk, about politics, about expert knowledge – than in the past? What new opportunities are there for forging new identities, new, more diverse forms of family and social relations, new forms of knowledge, on the Internet, through new media, different political groupings? What sort of structures influence people's experience – class, gender, 'race' and ethnicity?

Different aspects of social change are a key concern of sociology. It addresses the social structures that mark people out as different and are also sources of inequality, such as class, 'race' and gender. Sociology too engages with the debates about global changes, ranging from discussion of worldwide scale to those changes that take place in the private, personal areas of experience. Many of the debates which are the focus of sociological study are those which also permeate the other disciplines. Sociology draws attention to the interrelationship between the personal and the social and looks at how individuals fit into the societies within which they live in relation to the social structures, for example of gender, class, race and ethnicity at different levels and within different contexts.

Geography has a number of concerns that distinguish it from other social sciences. Firstly there is an interest in the distinctive character of places, and why they have developed in the way they have. Places are also unequal in wealth, power, unemployment and so on, and this makes a big difference to the way things develop culturally, economically and politically. Linked to this, there is interest in the uneven way places are connected together, and how globalization processes influence places in a variety of ways. Another concern of geography is to explore relationships between social change and the physical environment. Here there is concern not only with society's environmental impact, but also at the repercussions for society. This has assumed increased significance with concerns about the impact of new genetic technologies, and global environmental crisis. At several points in this book we have concentrated on place and the interconnections between place and other social, economic and political structures and some of the big debates which require attention to the specificities of location, for example in relation to identity, to race and ethnicity and to globalization. Another aspect of this dimension is space, for example as illustrated in our discussion of the relationship between the public and the private arenas, such as the separation at certain historical points between the public arena of decision making and of paid work and the private arena of relationships and domestic life.

Social policy provides a focus on many of the concerns of sociology but includes the specific focus on social institutions and welfare. These are informed by the concerns of other disciplines and interrelate with them but social policy retains a concentration upon the relationship between the state and social institutions and ways in which decision making impacts upon individuals and communities. Social institutions include those of family, work and welfare and encompass the ordering of everyday life as well as the institutions of state which structure experience. This is an area of change which impacts upon our everyday lives and is the subject of considerable debate within both the social sciences and popular culture.

All of these disciplines have been affected by changes in the world with which they have to engage in providing explanatory frameworks as well as policy recommendations. They all share a commitment to academic rigour and the need to support the claims that they make with adequate evidence. The social sciences are constantly developing and changing themselves, in response to changing times and to the questions that emerge from the research that is carried out. There are some shared areas of change, for example in the move towards a greater recognition of the importance of the ways in which culture mediates the processes involved in the production of knowledge. Increasingly, the disciplines which constitute the social sciences have drawn upon each other's research methods and major concerns and there has been a trend towards interdisciplinarity within many areas of the social sciences. Many of the issues raised in this book are the subject of major debates within each of the social science disciplines. Matters of identity, the impact of globalization, our perception of risk and the changes resulting from the expansion of the knowledge society are all subjects of interdisciplinary and discipline-specific interrogation.

Knowledge and the social sciences

Of course, this is only the start, but we have begun to pick out not only the debates, but also some of the key questions about the role of the social sciences. Knowledge is a diverse and multifaceted phenomenon. However it can be subdivided according to a number of factors, including what is being studied or discussed, the subject of knowledge, the way it is produced and the form it takes, that is how it is represented. In this book, I have concentrated on introducing some of the ways in which the social sciences produce knowledge about some of the big issues in our everyday lives. The subject is the social world. This has involved some exploration of knowledge produced at a number of different sites, ranging from those of popular culture, for example as represented in the media, fictional accounts and, of course, the sort of knowledge that is specific to the social sciences, such as that arising from empirical research, and which might be seen as having the status of expert knowledge. Social science knowledge demands systematic and rigorous investigation and draws upon evidence to support its claims, it involves the development of theoretical explanations which organize and frame the claims that are made.

It is, sometimes, difficult to disentangle some social science knowledge from what we might call everyday knowledge. There are many ways in which ideas and theories produced within the social sciences have infiltrated popular culture and everyday thinking. For example, the insights of psychoanalysis, drawing on Freud's theory of the unconscious, inform media discussions of self-help, problem pages, daytime television and our exchanges with our friends as well as more formal counselling and therapy. Some of the structures and concepts which have been used by social scientists to classify and organize their understanding of social phenomena have also been absorbed into everyday discourse, such as the notion of 'institutionalized racism', which prior to the Macpherson Report had been a term used mainly by sociologists. Media coverage of stock market crashes and alarm over mortgage repayments and pension funds, along with corporate scandals, brings the language of economics into the everyday.

However, at a time of enormous social, political and economic transformation there are other ways in which the social sciences contribute to changing forms of knowledge and to the changes that are taking place across the globe. The social sciences have never held the privileged elite position of other sources of expert knowledge, such as scientific, medical or religious knowledge, which have in the past achieved considerable authority and status, some of which remains, although these sources of expertise too have been challenged. The social sciences, in spite of the endeavours of some, earlier social scientists, have not largely laid claim to accessing some incontrovertible, objective truth. It has increasingly become the case that social scientists have pointed to the limitations of the claims that any discipline, including the natural and physical sciences, has access to truth. It can be argued that no method of inquiry and no research approach is value free or objective, however rigorous the use of experimentation and observation. All research involves some use of prejudged categories and concepts, some selection of both what is to be investigated and how knowledge will be produced. Thus 'objectivity' is an impossibility.

What can be achieved is research that conforms to the standards of the discipline, employs appropriate and rational criteria and recognized, well-supported methods. Research findings are then subject to the evaluation and assessment of peers within that area of study. The claims of the social sciences are invariably challenged by different theoretical explanations. However, this is not to say that their role and, especially, their transformative potential, is invalidated. Social science research, as we have seen in this book, provides an important source of information and analysis for governments, in the collection of data about populations and social trends as well as people's attitudes to change. Social science knowledges offer diverse and multifaceted understandings of social phenomena and of change which are necessary in a complex world where there have been significant shifts in sources of authority. The social sciences are able to engage with this diversity and complexity, to be flexible in responding to change and to provide frameworks and structures for making sense of the things that matter. Social science has been important in providing explanations and in identifying and defining the big issues in contemporary life. I hope this introduction to some of these ideas and ways of thinking makes you want to find out more!

Glossary

Agency   Action and energy which leads to activity on the part of human beings in directing the course of their own lives. Agency is often addressed in relation to structure, to indicate the tension between the choice and autonomy of individuals and groups, on the one hand, and the constraints of social and natural structures mostly outside their control, on the other. Whilst groups and individuals may be constrained by structures, those structures are also the product of human agency in many cases.

Capitalism   An economic system which is organized around the investment of private capital in large-scale production in the pursuit of profit. Capitalism can also be seen as a historically specific stage of economic development, in the Marxist critique, which focused particularly on its manifestations in nineteenth-century England, as the exploitative economic system whereby labour, as a commodity, produced profit for the bourgeoisie, the owners of the means of production, which followed feudalism.

Class   A large grouping of people who share common economic interests, experiences and lifestyles. This aspect of social divisions is linked to the economic and social organization of any society. Some social scientists give greater emphasis to the economic organization of production, especially in relation to ownership of the means of production or relegation to selling one's labour for a wage (Karl Marx). Others stress the importance of market position, that is occupation and the status that might be associated with different aspects of market position (Max Weber). Whatever the definition employed, class remains an important feature of social inequality. It is an issue which shapes social divisions in conjunction with other structures, such as gender, race and ethnicity with which class is deeply implicated.

Consumption   The process which involves the purchase of goods and services. Increasingly, it is argued that production and consumption are inextricably linked. The production of goods and services is influenced by patterns of consumption and consumer choice, as well as consumption being shaped by what is produced. There is a focus on the links between production and consumption which incorporates the importance of culture in the interaction of the whole process.

Cultural capital   The term was used by Pierre Bourdieu to describe social and cultural advantages which people are able to accrue as a result of their class position, for example the middle classes are able to access a more sophisticated use of language, knowledge, 'high' culture such as opera, literature and drama and the more high status sports such as golf. Working-class people tend to be limited to physical, body-based sports, for example boxing and have access to popular culture rather than more highly acclaimed cultural forms.

Diaspora   The dispersal of people across the globe, originally associated with the movement of Jewish people, but now used for a diverse range of people. It is also used as a category of identity, seen as particularly useful at a time of large-scale migration and to provide a means of explaining globalized identities and identities that cannot be traced to a single origin or home and often incorporate multiple sites of belonging. Diaspora is a concept used to understand globalized identities and citizenship, which cross the boundaries of the nation state, across the globe.

Difference   A relational concept, whereby something, or one group of people, is defined in terms of how it connects to something else or to another group. Difference can be oppositional, as in a binary opposition, good/bad, night/day, or it can relate to position in relation to other phenomena. For example Tuesday comes after Monday and before Wednesday. Binaries often involve a hierarchical opposition where one of the two is rated above the other.

Discourse   When deployed within the social sciences the term is often drawn from the work of Michel Foucault to go beyond the more common everyday meaning which focuses on language. For Foucault, it includes sets of ideas, practices, ways of producing knowledge and shaping what we do and think according to that specific knowledge. Truth is measured by the discourse itself, not by some external criteria. Thus a discourse is true if it is thought to be so.

Ethnicity   Identities may draw upon markers of visible difference and of physical characteristics but are based upon social features such as language, narratives, rituals and religion. Human societies are characterized by membership of ethnic groups, where ethnicity is not the same as nation and ethnicity transcends geographical boundaries and those of nation states. Thus an ethnic community would be a group of people whose shared identity is related to culture, history and/or language but whose relationship to territory and statehood might not be encompassed by a nation.

Gender   Many social scientists use the word gender to describe differences based on anatomical and physical characteristics associated with sexual difference. The term gender is preferred because it includes the social and cultural dimensions of difference. Gender is used to highlight the social construction of meanings about femininity and masculinity and the importance of social divisions between women and men. This focus on gender as implicated with sexual difference allows for an understanding of the social and political aspects of sex, rather than seeing sex and gender as separate and distinct.

Globalization   This is a social, cultural, political and economic phenomenon, which is subject to many different interpretations, ranging from those who see its impact as minimal and nothing new, to globalists or globalizers who argue that it is a recent and very significant phenomenon which has transformed life across the world. Some read this as a positive experience whilst others see it as having disastrous effects on local communities and those outside the western, especially US, mainstream. Most commentators agree that it has had some transforming impact.

Identification   A psychological process of association between oneself and something else, usually someone else. In the psychoanalytic work of Sigmund Freud the child identifies with the parent of the same sex and thus comes to take on the appropriate gender identity. Boys identify with their fathers and take in the attributes of masculinity. It is a psychological process and not simply a matter of copying behaviour.

Institutionalized racism   The systematic, structural and patterned forms of discrimination which operate at a range of different sites, based on race and ethnicity. This racism is generated by the organization, culture and attitudes of an institution or group.

Markets   In a market economy, resources are mainly allocated through exchange in markets. A market comprises all the exchanges involving a certain type of commodity.

Multicultural   A multicultural society is one in which civic nationalism and multi-ethnic citizenship are accompanied by public recognition, and participating citizens from a diversity of ethnic groups enjoy equal status and esteem.

Nation   A named and known people who recognize a solidarity and identity, which is the result of a common history, culture and sense of belonging to a common homeland. This can lead to feelings of nationalism, which involve emotive, affective identification with a political project to secure an independent nation state for the nation.

Nation state   A state which has external, fixed, recognized, demarcated borders and has some internal uniformity of rule and government.

Postmodernism   This school of thought has been associated with Jean Baudrillard, who is mentioned in this book, and other, often French, thinkers. In the social sciences, it refers to a set of theories that challenge modernism and the existence of universals, even the idea that there is a unified self, as well as other overarching structures, like social class. It counters the all-embracing approaches of the 'grand theories' such as Marxism, by suggesting that there is no single organizing framework of society, which is diverse and segmented. Such theories are often characterized by a focus on representation and culture and the myriad different ways in which meanings are produced and the fragmentation of contemporary societies.

Power   This is a much contested concept in the social sciences. It lies at the heart of social scientific enquiry in many fields as well as being fundamental to the exploration of social divisions and inequality as well as stratification, drawing on the work of Max Weber. Power can be seen as operating hierarchically from the top down or as more diffuse and present in all human exchanges. Michel Foucault argues that power is not only diffuse, but productive as well as illustrating constraint and even coercion. Power can be the power to do something as well as involving someone having the power to stop you doing something.

Production   The transformation of resources, such as raw materials, labour and time into goods and services. Considerable stress is placed on the efficiency of production, as productivity, in order to maximize profit and more recently upon the relationship between production and consumption in influencing productivity and decisions about what is produced. The outcome of a country's production is measured as its gross national product (GNP).

Race   The term race permits social scientists to stress the political significance of race and ethnicity and the use of 'race' in inverted commas shows that race is not a fixed biological category, but a dynamic, changing social concept. Race is not now used in the social sciences to describe biological make-up but the term is retained in order to hold onto the historical and political dimensions of this aspect of difference. Race, more than the term ethnicity, allows for a recognition of racism and racist practices which discriminate against people of different ethnicities.

Risk   Being exposed to dangerous situations and adverse conditions. Taking risks involves knowing that an action may prove costly and even dangerous. The magnitude of the risks that people take may be quite well known, for example thorough the availability of public information about them, or they may be unpredictable.

Risk society   One version of the state of contemporary societies which stresses changes in the ways in which awareness of risk, uncertainty and trust in expert sources of knowledge and advice changed in the latter part of the twentieth century. The risk society account emphasizes the importance of knowledge and perception of risk, especially in cultures where, although life expectancy has increased and standards of health and care have been vastly improved, there is still much more consciousness of risk and awareness of knowledge about possible risks and dangers.

Roles   The society into which we are born presents us with a series of roles, which are rather like parts in a play. The scripts are mostly already written, although, depending on our social and economic position and individual attributes, we can interpret these roles in different ways. A role comes with a pattern of behaviour, routines and responses. Although not the same as identities, roles offer a useful description of the social component of an identity. Development of theories about the significance of roles is associated with the work of Erving Goffman.

Social exclusion   Some groups are marginalized and cut off from full participation in social, political, economic and cultural life. These groups are not able to take full advantage of all that is available in these areas to the more affluent members of the society.

State The grouping of institutions which claim ultimate law-making authority over a particular territory. The state will also claim the monopoly on legitimate use of violence and coercion.

Status The honour, prestige or social standing which is associated with different groups in society. High status may or may not be accorded to those in social groups which have considerable wealth and does not derive necessarily from economic class position or occupation.

Structure This is used, often in conjunction with agency, to describe some of the organized or systematic, coherent constraints on human activity. Structures may take the form of social institutions, for example those of the state, or discourses which organize ideas and practices, like those of gender and ethnicity, or be based in physical or biological, embodied dimensions of experience. Structures are created and shaped by human agency in different ways at different times and in different contexts.

Symbolizing Making one word, object or image stand for another. For example green at the traffic lights means you can go and red means that you have to stop. The notion of symbolizing is used extensively in the social sciences as part of systems of representation through which we make sense of the world.

Taste A concept associated with the work of Pierre Bourdieu (1984) on the distinction between the different dispositions of people in particular social classes, such as taste in food and drink, clothes and leisure activities. Taste has specific social conditions, especially as derived from educational experience, which are linked to class.

Unconscious The unconscious mind is that part of the mind into which all the desires and feelings which we have had to suppress are deposited. For example when the small child's needs are not met the child represses these feelings into the unconscious. These feelings can emerge, often unexpectedly, later in life, for example in dreams, in jokes or in slips of the tongue. Thus dreams can be significant in revealing the feelings we have of which we are not otherwise conscious.

Further reading

Woodward, K. (ed.) (2004) *Questioning Identity, Gender, Class, Ethnicity*, London: Routledge.

Hinchliffe, S. and Woodward, K. (eds) (2004) *The Natural and the Social: Uncertainty, Risk, Change*, London: Routledge.

Hughes, G. and Fergusson, R. (eds) (2004) *Ordering Lives: Family, Work, Welfare*, London: Routledge.

Held, D. (ed.) (2004) *A Globalizing World? Culture, Economics, Politics*, London: Routledge.

Goldblatt, D. (ed.) (2004) *Knowledge and the Social Sciences: Theory, Method, Practice*, London: Routledge.

These books form part of the Open University courses DD100, DD121 and DD122, An Introduction to the Social Sciences: Understanding Social Change. For more information contact http://www.open/ac.uk or Call Centre, PO Box 724, The Open University, Milton Keynes MK7 6ZS, UK.

Bibliography

Abu-Habib, L. (2002) 'Welfare, Rights and the Disability Movement' in Grewal and Kaplan.

Adam, B. (2002) 'The gendered time politics of globalization: of shadowlands and elusive justice', *Feminist Review*, 70: 3–29.

Ahmed, K. (2002) 'The boy on the left had no future. The one on the right is a talented star pupil', *The Observer*, 13 October.

Allucquere, R. S. (2000) 'Will the Real Body Please Stand Up? Boundary Stories about Virtual Culture' in Bell and Kennedy.

American Foreign Policy Association (2002) Globalization's Last Hurrah? <www.globalpolicy.org.globaliz/define/0101.htm>

Anderson, B. ([1983] 1991) *Imagined Communities: Reflections on the Origins and Spread of Nationalism*, 2nd edn, London: Verso.

Armstrong, G. and Giulianotti, R. (1999) *Football Cultures and Identities*, Basingstoke: Macmillan.

Arnot, C. (2002) 'Pride and prejudice', *Manchester Guardian*, 24 July, pp. 2–3.

Balsamo, A. (2000) 'The Virtual Body in Cyberspace' in Bell and Kennedy.

Barthes, R. (1972) *Mythologies*, London: Cape.

— (1977) *Image – Music – Text*, Glasgow: Fontana.

Baudrillard, J. (1988) 'Consumer Society' in Poster, M. (ed.) *Selected Writings*, Cambridge: Polity.

Bauman, Z. (1987) *Legislators and Interpreters. On Modernity, Postmodernity and Intellectuals*, Cambridge: Polity.

— (2001) 'Survival as a social construct', *Theory, Culture and Society*, 9: 1–36.

Bauman, Z. and May, T. ([1990] 2001) *Thinking Sociologically*, Oxford: Blackwell.

Bayoumi, M. and Rubin, A. (eds) (2001) *The Edward Said Reader*, London: Granta.

Beck, U. (1992) *Risk Society: Towards a New Modernity*, London: Sage.

Bell, D. (1976) *The Cultural Contradictions of Capitalism*, London: Heinemann.

Bell, D. and Kennedy, N. (eds) (2000) *The Cybercultures Reader*, London: Routledge.

Berger, J. (1984) *And Our Faces, My Heart, Brief as Photos*, London: Writers and Readers.

Beveridge, W. (1942) *Social Insurance and Allied Services* [The Beveridge Report], Cm. 6404, London: HMSO.

Bhavnani, K. K. (1993) 'Towards a multicultural Europe?: "race", nation and identity in 1992 and beyond', *Feminist Review*, 45: 30–45.

Bhavnani, K. K. and Coulson, M. (1986) 'Transforming socialist feminism: the challenge of racism', *Feminist Review*, 23: 81–92.

Bocock, R. (1982) *Freud*, London: Tavistock.

Bonnett, A. (1998) 'Constructions of Whiteness in European and American Anti Racism' in Werbner, P. and Modood, T. (eds) *Debating Cultural Hybridity*, London: Zed Books.

Bourdieu, P. (1986) *Distinction: A Social Critique of the Judgement of Taste*, London: Routledge.

Brah, A. (1993) 'Re-framing Europe: engendered racisms ethnicities and nationalisms in contemporary Western Europe', *Feminist Review*, 45: 9–29.

Branwyn, G. (2000) 'Compu. Sex Erotica for Cybernauts' in Bell and Kennedy.

Callinicos, A. (2000) *Equality*, Cambridge: Polity.

Carvel, J. (2002) 'The Census', *The Guardian*, 1 October, p. 4.

Castells, M. (1996) *The Rise of the Network Society*, Oxford: Blackwell.

— (1997) *The Power of Identity*, Oxford: Blackwell.

Collins, P. Hill (1990) *Black Feminist Thought: Knowledge, Consciousness and the Politics of Empowerment*, New York: Routledge.

Connell, R. W. (1985) *Masculinities*, Berkeley: University of California.

Corker, M. and Shakespeare, T. (2002) 'Disability/Postmodernism' in Corker, M. and Shakespeare, T. (eds) *Embodying Disability Theory*, London: Continuum.

Davis-Floyd, R. and Dumit, J. (eds) (1998) *Cyborg Babies: From Techno-Sex to Techno-Tots*, London: Routledge.

Department of Social Security (1998) *Households Below Average Income: A Statistical Analysis 1979–1995/6*, London: The Stationery Office.

Donzelot, J. (1980) *The Policing of Families*, London: Hutchinson.

du Gay, P., Hall, S., Janes, L., Mackay, H. and Negus, K. (eds) (1997) *Doing Cultural Studies*, Buckingham: Open University Press.

Durkheim, E. (1915) *The Elementary Forms of the Religious Life: A Study in Religious Sociology*, trans. J. Swain, London: Allen and Unwin.

— (1964) *The Division of Labour in Society*, New York: Free Press.

Dyer, C. (2003) 'Judge backs adoption of IVF mix-up twins', *The Guardian*, 27 February, p. 2.

Eisenstein, Z. (1981) *The Radical Future of Liberal Feminism*, New York: Longman.

Falk, P. (1994) *The Consuming Body*, London: Sage.

Featherstone, M. (1991) *Consumer Culture and Postmodernmism*, London: Sage.

— (2000) 'Post-bodies, Ageing and Virtual Reality' in Bell and Kennedy.

Feuer, L. (ed.) (1959) *Marx and Engels. Basic Writings on Politics and Philosophy*, New York: Anchor Doubleday.

Foucault, M. (1981) *The History of Sexuality*, Vol. 1, New York: Vintage.

— (1988) 'Technologies of the Self' in Martin, L., Gutman, H. and Hutton, P. (eds) *Technologies of the Self: A Seminar with Michel Foucault*, Amherst, MA: University of Massachussetts Press.

Frankenburg, R. (1993) *White Women and Race Matters. The Social Construction of Whiteness*, Minneapolis: University of Minnesota Press.

Freud, S. (1905) *The Interpretation of Dreams*, trans. J. Strachey, 1965, New York: Avon Books.

Friedman, T. L. (1999) *The Lexus and the Olive Tree*, New York: Farrar, Strauss and Giroux.

Galbraith, J. K. ([1999] 2002) The Crisis of Globalization <www.igc.apc.org/dissent/current/summer99/galbrait.html>

Gellner, E. (1983) *Nations and Nationalism*, Oxford: Blackwell.

Gerth, H. and Mills, C. (1948) *From Marx to Weber*, London: Routledge.

Giddens, A. (1991) *Modernity and Self-Identity: Self and Society in the late Modern Age*, Oxford: Polity.

— (1992) *The Transformation of Intimacy: Sexuality, Love and Eroticism in Modern Societies*, Cambridge: Polity.

— ([1999] 2002) *Runaway World, The Reith Lectures, 1999*, 2nd edn, London: Profile Books.

Gilroy, P. (1992) 'The End of Anti-racism' in Donald, J. and Rattansi, A. (eds) *'Race', Culture and Difference*, London: Sage.

Goffman, E. (1959) *The Presentation of Self in Everyday Life*, New York: Doubleday.

— (1963) *Stigma: Notes on the Management of Spoiled Identity*, Englewood Cliffs, NJ: Prentice Hall.

Goldberg, D. T. and Quayson, A. (eds) (2002) *Relocating Postcolonialism*, Oxford: Blackwell.

Goldblatt, D. (2002) *World Football Year Book*, London: Dorling Kindersley.

Goodley, D. and Rapley, M. (2002) 'People with Learning Disabilities' in Corker and Shakespeare.

Grewal, I. and Kaplan, C. (eds) (2002) *An Introduction to Women's Studies*, New York: McGraw Hill.

<Guardian.co.uk/Britain>

Hall, S. (1991) 'The Local and the Global' in King, A. D. (ed.) *Culture, Globalisation and the World System*, London: Macmillan.

— (1992a) 'The Question of Cultural Identity' in Hall, S., Held, D. D. and McGrew, T. (eds) *Modernity and its Futures*, Cambridge: Polity with Blackwell Publishers and the Open University.

— (1992b) 'The West and the Rest' in Hall, S. and Gieben, B. (eds) *Formation of Modernity*, Cambridge: Polity with the Open University.

— (1995) 'New Culture for Old' in Massey, D. and Jess, P. (eds) *A Place in the World: Places, Culture and Globalization*, Oxford: Oxford University Press.

— (ed.) (1997) *Representation: Cultural Representations and Signifying Practices*, London: Sage.

Hammonds, E. M. (2002) 'New Technologies of Race' in Grewal and Kaplan.

Haraway, D. (1997) 'The Virtual Speculum in the New World Order', *Feminist Review*, 55, Spring.

— (1998) 'The Persistence of Vision' in Mirzoeff, N. (ed.) *Visual Culture Reader*, London: Routledge.

— [1985] (2000) 'A Manifesto for Cyborgs' in Kirkup et al.

Hawkes, T. (1988) *Structuralism and Semiotics*, London: Routledge.

Held, D. (2000) *A Globalizing World? Culture, Economics, Politics*, London: Routledge.

Held, D. and McGrew, A. (eds) (2000) *The Global Transformations Reader*, Cambridge: Polity.

Held, D., McGrew, A., Goldbatt, D. and Perraton, J. (1999) *Global Transformations*, Cambridge: Polity.

Henley Centre, The (2000) Blurring Demographics <www.henleycentre.com>

Hochschild, A. (1994) 'The commercial spirit of intimate life and the abduction of feminism: signs from women's advice books', *Theory, Culture and Society*, 11: 1–24.

Ignatieff, M. (1993) 'The highway of brotherhood and unity', *Granta*, 45: 225–43.

— (1994) *Nationalism and the Narcissism of Minor Differences*, Milton Keynes: Open University Press, Centre Paper.

Jackson, S. and Scott, S. (eds) (2002) *Gender: A Sociological Reader*, London: Routledge.

Jamieson, L. (1998) *Intimacy: Personal Relationships in Modern Societies*, Cambridge: Polity.

Jarvis, M. (ed.) (2002) *Poems for Refugees*, London: Vintage.

Jenkins, R. (1996) *Social Identity*, London: Routledge.

Jordan, T. and Pile, S. (eds) (2002) *Social Change*, Oxford: Blackwell.

Kaplan, E. A. (1992) *Motherhood and Representation: The Mother in Popular Culture and Melodrama*, London: Routledge.

Kirkup, G., Janes, L., Woodward, K. and Hovenden, F. (eds) (2000) *The Gendered Cyborg*, London: Routledge.

Klein, N. (2001) *No Logo*, London: Flamingo.

Lasn, K. (2000) 'Culture Jamming' in Schor, J. and Holt, D. (eds) *The Consumer Society Reader*, New York: The New Press.

Leadbeater, C. (1999) *Living on Thin Air: The New Economy*, London: Viking.

Lee, D. (2002) 'IVF twins mix-up poses complex questions for family courts', *The Times, Law*, 16 July.

Lee, S. (1993) 'Racial classifications in the US census 1890–1990', *Ethnic and Racial Studies*, 16 (1): 75–94.

Lutz, H. (2002) 'At your service madam? The globalization of domestic service', *Feminist Review*, 70: 89–104.

Macpherson, W. (1999) The Stephen Lawrence Inquiry. Report of an Inquiry by Sir William Macpherson of Cluny, Cm 4262–I, London: The Stationery Office.

Marshall, T. H. (1964) *Class, Citizenship and Social Development*, Cambridge: Cambridge University Press.

— ([1964] 1994) 'Citizenship and Class' in Turner, B. S. and Hamilton, P. (eds) *Citizenship: Critical Concepts*, Vol. 2, London: Routledge, pp. 5–44.

Marx, K. and Engels, F. (1959) *The Communist Manifesto*, in Feuer, L. (ed.) *Marx and Engels. Basic Writings on Politics and Philosophy*, New York: Anchor Doubleday.

Mead, G. H. (1934) *Mind, Self and Society*, Chicago: University of Chicago Press.

Mercer, K. (1990) 'Welcome to the Jungle' in Rutherford.

Miller, D. (1995) *Acknowledging Consumption*, London: Routledge.

— (1997) 'Consumption and its Consequences' in Mackay, H. (ed.) *Consumption and Everyday Life*, London: Sage.

Moore, H. (1994) *A Passion for Difference: Essays in Anthropology and Gender*, Cambridge: Polity.

Oakley, A. (1972) *Sex, Gender and Society*, London: Temple Smith.

Nelson, B. (1995) Introduction to *The Ladies' Paradise* vii–xxiv, Zola ([1883] 1995).

Nicholson, L. (1992) 'Feminist Theory: The Private and the Public' in McDowell, L. and Pringle, R. (eds) *Defining Women*, Cambridge: Polity.

Parekh, B. (2000a) *The Future of Multi Ethnic Britain, The Parekh Report*, London: Profile Books.

— (2000b) *Rethinking Multi Culturalism: Cultural Diversity and Political Theory*, Basingstoke: Macmillan.

Parker, T. (1994) *May the Lord in His Mercy be Kind to Belfast*, London: Harper Collins.

Pateman, C. (1988) *The Sexual Contract*, Cambridge: Polity.

Petchesky, R. ([1985] 2000) 'Foetal Imaging' in Kirkup et al.

Petchesky, R. and Judd, K. (eds) (1998) *Negotiating Reproductive Rights*, London: Zed Books.

Phizacklea, A. (1998) 'Migration and Globalization, A Feminist Perspective' in Koser, K. and Lutz, H. (eds) (1998) *The New Migration in Europe, Social Construction and Social Realities*, London and Basingstoke: Macmillan.

Potts, L. (1990) *The World Labour Market: A History of Migration*, trans. Terry Bond, London: Zed Books.

— (2002) 'Excerpt from *The World Labour Market: A History of Migration*' in Grewal and Kaplan, pp. 440–3.

Poverty and Social Exclusion Survey of Britain (1999) Joseph Rowntree Foundation.

Richardson, D. (2000) *Rethinking Sexuality*, London: Sage.

Rose, G. (1990) 'Place and Identity: A Sense of Place' in Massey, D. and Jess, P. (eds) *A Place in the World?* Oxford: Oxford University Press.

Rothman, P. (1992) 'Feminism, Subjectivity and Sexual Difference' in Gunew, S. (ed.) *Feminist Knowledge: Critique and Construct*, London: Routledge.

Roux, C. (2002) 'The reign of Spain', *The Guardian*, 28 October, pp. 6–7.

Rutherford, J. (ed.) (1990) *Identity, Community, Culture, Difference*, London: Lawrence and Wishart.

Said, E. (1978) *Orientalism*, Harmondsworth: Penguin.

Sarup, M. (1996) *Identity, Culture and the PostModern World*, Edinburgh: Edinburgh University Press.

Sassen, S. (1998) *Globalization and the Discounts: Essays on the New Mobilities of People and Money*, New York: The New Press.

— (2001) 'A message from the global south', *Manchester Guardian*, 12 September.

Scheper-Hughes, N. (1992) *Death without Weeping: The Violence of Everyday Life in Brazil*, Berkeley/Los Angeles: University of California Press.

Shakespeare, T. (1994) 'Cultural representation of disabled people: dustbins for disavowel?', *Disability and Society*, 9 (3): 183–99.

Shilling, C. (1997) 'The Body and Difference' in Woodward.

Shiva, V. (2002) *Poverty and Globalization* (The Reith Lectures), London: BBC, <http://news.bbc.co.uk/hi/english/static/events/reith –2000/lecture5.stm>

Skeggs, B. (1997) *Formations of Class and Identity*, London: Sage.

Social Exclusion Unit (2000) *National Strategy for Urban Renewal*, CM4045, London: The Stationery Office.

Social Trends (2002) London: HMSO.

Spittle, S. (2002) 'Producing TV: Consuming TV' in Miles, S., Anderson, A. and Meethan, K. (eds) *The Changing Consumer: Markets and Meanings*, London: Routledge.

Squires, J. (2002) 'Public and Private' in Grewal and Kaplan, pp. 166–9.

Stacey, J. (2000) 'The Global Within' in Franklin, S., Lury, C. and Stacey, J. (eds) *Global Nature, Global Culture*, London: Sage, pp. 97–145.

Steans, J. (2000) 'The Gender Dimension' in Held and McGrew.

Thompson, G. (2000) 'Economic Globalization?' in Held.

Thomson, R. G. (2002) 'Theorizing Disability' in Golberg and Quayson, pp. 231–69.

Trinh Minh-Ha (1992) *Framer Framed*, New York: Routledge.

Tsang, D. (2000) 'Notes on Queer "N" Asian Virtual Sex' in Bell and Kennedy.

Twine, F. (1994) *Citizenship and Social Rights: The Interdependence of Self and Society*, London: Sage.

Urry, J. (2000) *Sociology beyond Societies: Mobilities for the Twenty-first Century*, London: Routledge.

— (2002) The Media and the War on Terrorism, *Pavis Lecture*, Milton Keynes: Open University.

Visvanathan, N., Duggan, L., Nisonoff, L. and Weigersman, N. (eds) (1997) *The Women, Gender and Development Reader*, London: Zed Books.

Wakeford, N. (2000) 'Cyberqueer' in Bell and Kennedy.

Warren, J. W. and Twine, F. W. (1997) 'White Americans: The New Minority?', *Journal of Black Studies*, 28 (2): 200–18.

Wiley, J. (1999) 'Nobody is Doing It: Cybersexuality' in Price, J. and Shildrick, M. (eds) *Feminist Theory and the Body*, Edinburgh: Edinburgh University Press.

Wilson, A. and Beresford, P. (2002) 'Madness, Distress and Postmodernity: Putting the Record Straight' in Corker and Shakespeare.

Wilson, E. (1977) *Women and the Welfare State*, London: Tavistock.

— (2001) *The Contradictions of Culture: Cities, Culture, Women*, London: Sage.

Wilson, R. M. S., Gilligan, C. and Pearson, D. (1992) *Strategic Marketing Management*, London: The Stationery Office.

Woodward, K. (ed.) (1997a) *Identity and Difference*, London: Sage.

— (1997b) 'Concepts of Identity and Difference' in Woodward.

— (1997c) 'Motherhood: Meanings and Myths' in Woodward.

— (2000a) *Questioning Identity*, London: Routledge.

— (2000b) 'Representing Reproduction: Reproducing Representation' in Kirkup et al.

— (2000c) Defining Moments BBC, Open University TV programme.

— (2002) 'Up Close and Personal: The Changing Face of Intimacy' in Jordan and Pile.

Woolf, J. (1985) 'The invisible flaneuse: women and the literature of modernity', *Theory, Culture and Society*, 2 (3): 44–68.

Wroe, M. (2002) 'In Cyberspace we all put on an Act' *Sunday Times*, Section 9, 25 August.

Zola, E. ([1883] 1995) *The Ladies' Paradise*, trans. Brian Nelson, Oxford: Oxford University Press.

Index

Woodward uses a poem by Jackie Kay to/as an example of both the complexity intrachanced id + strength of feeling granted by an individual